Psychoanalysis as Therapy and Storytelling

Psychoanalysis as Therapy and Storytelling examines psychoanalysis from two perspectives – as a cure for psychic suffering, and as a series of stories between patient and analyst.

Antonino Ferro uses numerous clinical examples to investigate how narration and interpretation are interconnected in the analytic session. He draws on and develops Bion's theories to present a novel perspective on subjects such as:

- Psychoanalysis as a particular form of literature
- Sexuality as a narrative genre or dialect in the analyst's consulting room
- Delusion and hallucination
- Acting out, the countertransference and the transgenerational field
- Play: characters, narrations and interpretations

Psychoanalytic clinicians and theoreticians alike will find the innovative approach to the analytic session described here of great interest.

Antonino Ferro is Full Member of the Italian Psychoanalytical Association and the IPA. He is a child and adolescent psychoanalyst and is especially concerned with adults with serious pathologies. His previous publications with Routledge include *Seeds of Illness, Seeds of Recovery*, *In the Analyst's Consulting Room* and *The Bi-personal Field.*

THE NEW LIBRARY OF PSYCHOANALYSIS
General Editor Dana Birksted-Breen

The New Library of Psychoanalysis was launched in 1987 in association with the Institute of Psychoanalysis, London. It took over from the International Psychoanalytical Library, which published many of the early translations of the works of Freud and the writings of most of the leading British and Continental psychoanalysts.

The purpose of the New Library of Psychoanalysis is to facilitate a greater and more widespread appreciation of psychoanalysis and to provide a forum for increasing mutual understanding between psychoanalysts and those working in other disciplines such as the social sciences, medicine, philosophy, history, linguistics, literature and the arts. It aims to represent different trends both in British psychoanalysis and in psychoanalysis generally. The New Library of Psychoanalysis is well placed to make available to the English-speaking world psychoanalytic writings from other European countries and to increase the interchange of ideas between British and American psychoanalysts.

The Institute, together with the British Psychoanalytical Society, runs a low-fee psychoanalytic clinic, organizes lectures and scientific events concerned with psychoanalysis and publishes the *International Journal of Psychoanalysis*. It also runs the only UK training course in psychoanalysis that leads to membership of the International Psychoanalytical Association – the body which preserves internationally agreed standards of training, of professional entry, and of professional ethics and practice for psychoanalysis as initiated and developed by Sigmund Freud. Distinguished members of the Institute have included Michael Balint, Wilfred Bion, Ronald Fairbairn, Anna Freud, Ernest Jones, Melanie Klein, John Rickman and Donald Winnicott.

ALSO IN THIS SERIES

Impasse and Interpretation Herbert Rosenfeld
Psychoanalysis and Discourse Patrick Mahony
The Suppressed Madness of Sane Men Marion Milner
The Riddle of Freud Estelle Roith
Thinking, Feeling, and Being Ignacio Matte-Blanco
The Theatre of the Dream Salomon Resnik
Melanie Klein Today: Volume 1, Mainly Theory Edited by Elizabeth Bott Spillius
Melanie Klein Today: Volume 2, Mainly Practice Edited by Elizabeth Bott Spillius
Psychic Equilibrium and Psychic Change: Selected Papers of Betty Joseph Edited by Michael Feldman and Elizabeth Bott Spillius
About Children and Children-No-Longer: Collected Papers 1942–80 Paula Heimann. Edited by Margret Tonnesmann
The Freud–Klein Controversies 1941–45 Edited by Pearl King and Riccardo Steiner
Dream, Phantasy and Art Hanna Segal
Psychic Experience and Problems of Technique Harold Stewart
Clinical Lectures on Klein and Bion Edited by Robin Anderson
From Fetus to Child Alessandra Piontelli
A Psychoanalytic Theory of Infantile Experience: Conceptual and Clinical Reflections E Gaddini. Edited by Adam Limentani
The Dream Discourse Today Edited and introduced by Sara Flanders
The Gender Conundrum: Contemporary Psychoanalytic Perspectives on Femininity and Masculinity Edited and introduced by Dana Breen
Psychic Retreats John Steiner
The Taming of Solitude: Separation Anxiety in Psychoanalysis Jean-Michel Quinodoz
Unconscious Logic: An Introduction to Matte-Blanco's Bi-logic and Its Uses Eric Rayner
Understanding Mental Objects Meir Perlow
Life, Sex and Death: Selected Writings of William Gillespie Edited and introduced by Michael Sinason
What Do Psychoanalysts Want? The Problem of Aims in Psychoanalytic Therapy Joseph Sandler and Anna Ursula Dreher
Michael Balint: Object Relations, Pure and Applied Harold Stewart
Hope: A Shield in the Economy of Borderline States Anna Potamianou
Psychoanalysis, Literature and War: Papers 1972–1995 Hanna Segal
Emotional Vertigo: Between Anxiety and Pleasure Danielle Quinodoz
Early Freud and Late Freud Ilse Grubrich-Simitis
A History of Child Psychoanalysis Claudine and Pierre Geissmann
Belief and Imagination: Explorations in Psychoanalysis Ronald Britton

A Mind of One's Own: A Kleinian View of Self and Object Robert A. Caper
Psychoanalytic Understanding of Violence and Suicide Edited by Rosine Jozef Perelberg
On Bearing Unbearable States of Mind Ruth Riesenberg-Malcolm
Psychoanalysis on the Move: The Work of Joseph Sandler Edited by Peter Fonagy, Arnold M. Cooper and Robert S. Wallerstein
The Dead Mother: The Work of André Green Edited by Gregorio Kohon
The Fabric of Affect in the Psychoanalytic Discourse André Green
The Bi-Personal Field: Experiences of Child Analysis Antonino Ferro
The Dove that Returns, the Dove that Vanishes: Paradox and Creativity in Psychoanalysis Michael Parsons
Ordinary People and Extra-Ordinary Protections: A Post-Kleinian Approach to the Treatment of Primitive Mental States Judith Mitrani
The Violence of Interpretation: From Pictogram to Statement Piera Aulagnier
The Importance of Fathers: A Psychoanalytic Re-Evaluation Judith Trowell and Alicia Etchegoyen
Dreams That Turn Over a Page: Paradoxical Dreams in Psychoanalysis Jean-Michel Quinodoz
The Couch and the Silver Screen: Psychoanalytic Reflections on European Cinema Edited and introduced by Andrea Sabbadini
In Pursuit of Psychic Change: The Betty Joseph Workshop Edited by Edith Hargreaves and Arturo Varchevker
The Quiet Revolution in American Psychoanalysis: Selected Papers of Arnold M. Cooper Arnold M. Cooper. Edited and introduced by Elizabeth L. Auchincloss
Seeds of Illness, Seeds of Recovery: The Genesis of Suffering and the Role of Psychoanalysis Antonino Ferro
The Work of Psychic Figurability: Mental States Without Representation César Botella and Sára Botella
Key Ideas for a Contemporary Psychoanalysis: Misrecognition and Recognition of the Unconscious André Green
The Telescoping of Generations: Listening to the Narcissistic Links Between Generations Haydé Faimberg
Glacial Times: A Journey Through the World of Madness Salomon Resnik
This Art of Psychoanalysis: Dreaming Undreamt Dreams and Interrupted Cries Thomas H. Ogden
Psychoanalysis as Therapy and Storytelling Antonio Ferro
Psychoanalysis in the 21st Century: Competitors or Collaborators? Edited by David M. Black

TITLES IN THE NEW LIBRARY OF PSYCHOANALYSIS TEACHING SERIES

Reading Freud: A Chronological Exploration of Freud's Writings Jean-Michel Quinodoz

THE NEW LIBRARY OF PSYCHOANALYSIS

General Editor: Dana Birksted-Breen

Psychoanalysis as Therapy and Storytelling

Antonino Ferro

Translated by Philip Slotkin

The translation of this work has been part-funded by SEPS
Segretariato Europeo per le Pubblicazioni Scientifiche

SEPS
SEGRETARIATO EUROPEO PER LE PUBBLICAZIONI SCIENTIFICHE

Via Val d'Aposa 7 – 40123 Bologna – Italy
tel +39 051 271992 – fax +39 051 265983
seps@alma.unibo.it – www.seps.it

Routledge
Taylor & Francis Group
LONDON AND NEW YORK

First published 1999 as *La psicoanalisi come letteratura e terapia* by
Raffaello Cortina Editore, Milan

English language edition first published 2006 by Routledge
27 Church Road, Hove, East Sussex, BN3 2FA

Simultaneously published in the USA and Canada
by Routledge
270 Madison Avenue, New York, NY 10016

Routledge is an imprint of the Taylor & Francis Group

Typeset in Bembo by Keystroke, Jacaranda Lodge, Wolverhampton
Printed and bound in Great Britain by TJ International Ltd, Padstow, Cornwall
Paperback cover design by Sandra Heath

This publication has been produced with paper manufactured to strict environmental standards and with pulp derived from sustainable forests.

British Library Cataloguing in Publication Data
A catalogue record for this book is available from the British Library

Library of Congress Cataloging in Publication Data
Ferro, Antonino, 1947–
[Psicoanalisi come letteratura e terapia. English]
Psychoanalysis as therapy and storytelling / Antonino Ferro ;
translated by Philip Slotkin.
p. cm. -- (The new library of psychoanalysis)
Includes bibliographical references and index.
ISBN-13: 978-0-415-37204-6 (hbk)
ISBN-10: 0-415-37204-6 (hbk)
ISBN-13: 978-0-415-37205-3 (pbk.)
ISBN-10: 0-415-37205-4 (pbk.)
1. Psychoanalysis. 2. Psychotherapist and patient. 3. Psychoanalysis and literature. I. Title. II. Series: New library of psychoanalysis (Unnumbered)
[DNLM: 1. Psychoanalytic Therapy--methods. 2. Narration. 3. Psychoanalytic Interpretation. 4. Professional-Patient Relations. 5. Medicine in Literature. WM 460.6 F395p 2006a]
RC504.F52713 2006
616.89'17--dc22

2006001875

ISBN13: 978–0–415–37204–6 (hbk)
ISBN13: 978–0–415–37205–3 (pbk)

ISBN10: 0–415–37204–6 (hbk)
ISBN10: 0–415–37205–4 (pbk)

For Product Safety Concerns and Information please contact our EU representative: GPSR@taylorandfrancis.com.
Taylor & Francis Verlag GmbH, Kaufingerstraße 24, 80331 München, Germany.

Translated by Philip Slotkin

Title of original Italian edition: *La psicoanalisi come letteratura e terapia*

riverrum, past Eve and
Adam's . . . brings us . . .
back to Howth Castle and Environs.

James Joyce

Contents

1

Narrations and interpretations

The term 'narration', as used in psychoanalysis, is highly ambiguous, because its semantic halo is either excessively predefined or too wide-ranging. The following possibilities may be considered: (a) 'Narration' can be understood as the stories told by patients during analysis in relation to their family romance or, if you will, their internal world. (b) It can be understood symmetrically as the interventions in which, say, the analyst undertakes an extension into the world of 'myth' (Bion 1963),[1] when he recounts something meaningful from a position on Row C of the Grid.[2] (c) It can be understood as referring to a particular quality of the analyst's interpretations, when they are especially open and unsaturated, and instead of closing off the sense allow for its further expansion (*narrative interpretations* – Ferro 1996a). (d) It can be understood as the use, outside the sessions, of a story or play particularly suited to the illustration of psycho-analytic-type implications – for example, Freud's use of the story of the sinister Sand-Man or the theme of the three caskets. (e) Finally, it can be understood as the construction of a narrative truth (Spence 1982) instead of an unknowable historical truth.

Although my own use of the term may, to some extent and at certain points, marginally overlap the above possibilities, for me it denotes something quite different: by narration *I mean a way of being in the session whereby the analyst shares with the patient in the 'construction of a meaning' on a strongly dialogic basis, without particular interpretative caesuras.* It is as if analyst and patient were together constructing a drama within which the various plots increase in complexity, intersect and develop, sometimes even in ways that are unpredictable and unthinkable for the two co-narrators, neither of whom is a 'strong' holder of a preconstituted truth. Within this mode of proceeding, *co-narrative transformation* or indeed *transformational co-narration* takes the place of interpretation (Ferro 1997c).[3]

For me it is an open question whether a sense-saturating interpretation may be useful at a certain point. My analytic superego or ego ideal often says yes, while 'taste' and respect for creativity suggest a negative answer, because this decoding of a 'true truth' reminds me of the kind of interpretations given by certain critics who claim to reveal the true meaning of a work of art.

Co-narrative transformation, and to an even greater extent transformational co-narration, resulting from genuine dialogic cooperation between patient and analyst are therefore the offspring of the minds of both; they generate new and open senses, and do not impose an excessive burden on the parts or modes of functioning of the patient that are not yet capable of full receptivity and dependence (Di Chiara 1992).

There is a well-known Jewish anecdote about a boy from a poor family who is sent to school by his parents at great financial sacrifice. After a few days, he categorically proclaims that he does not wish to continue. Questioned about this decision by his astonished father, he eventually replies: 'Because at school they teach me things I don't know.' This in my view illustrates the level of the problem, which not only *can* be avoided by recourse to a co-narration, but also *must* be avoided because *in analysis there is no one holder of preconstituted truths about the patient* (if there were, we should be in –K and Column 2),[4] but instead a sense that can be developed only by con-sensus (development of ♀♂, of ♀ and of ♂).

The characters of narrations have a status (indeed, so too does the entire discourse) that extends from a very high degree of real, historical referentiality (as in a psychologistic reading of the characters of, say, Manzoni's *The Betrothed*), via characters centred on themselves as aspects and parts of an internal dialogue (e.g. James Joyce's *Ulysses*), to a complexity of semantic articulations, transformations and open senses in a state of continuous becoming, as in Joyce's other literary miracle, *Finnegans Wake*.

Co-narration is the form in which analyst and patient 'dance' along Row C of the Grid until they are able – where this proves possible – to move on from C to D, and so on.

A seeming digression: towards a clinical model

I use the term 'model' as a provisional truth, validating it to a greater or lesser extent according to the number of problems it helps me to solve. In other words, I regard it as a provisional, unsaturated narration: I do not ask myself whether I am in the presence of β-elements, an α-function or α-elements, but see this as a way of narrating mental functioning that I find useful for arriving at a satisfactory solution to problems on the mental and emotional level. However, I am prepared to use any other model that may ultimately prove suitable, or more suitable, for this purpose.

In Bion's model, the most serious pathologies can be associated with a dearth (or even a total absence) of α-function and a hyperpresence of β-elements which, finding no possibility of transformation, are continuously evacuated in various ways.

The focal point is therefore not so much the accumulation of β as the lack of an α-function, due to the very early failure of 'social' relations that has precluded the introjection of the α-function, the primordial constituent of any kind of mental life.

The disturbance in the formation of α is not always complete; there is a gradient of possibilities. If the α-function is minimally operational, the patient may exhibit *panic attack* syndromes (Ferro 1996a). I call this the 'Krakatoa syndrome',[5] because it results from a sudden eruption of β-elements – proto-emotions – which, in the absence of a 'stream-bed' as represented by an α-function capable of receiving and transforming them, flood the mind to devastating effect.

Such patients require a maximum degree of constancy of the setting, because any change activates the agglutinated nuclei (Bleger 1966) which are stratified in the setting itself (pockets of β-elements) and which may once again burst on to the scene. These patients are constantly on the look-out for any change in the analyst's mental life, which to them is like a semi-permeable dam against the agglutinated nuclei, and which can transform them by means of the system of sluices (progressive alphabetizations) into building blocks of thought (α-elements). If the 'dam' shows signs of malfunctioning, the result downstream is of course panic, because this foreshadows the possibility of a flood.

In intrapsychic terms, we have a marginally adequate α-function, which, however, being inefficient, is periodically overwhelmed by conglomerates of β-elements. These conglomerates, which have previously been described as 'betalomas' (Barale and Ferro 1992), may be likened on the visual level to the eponymous blob of jelly in Irvin S. Yeaworth Jr's extraordinary 1958 film *The Blob*, an entity that falls to earth from an asteroidal fragment and starts devouring everything, assuming more and more dimensions as it goes: nothing can stop the blob until it is discovered that cold can freeze it solid. The number of possible psychoanalytic exercises on this subject, and of possible interpretations of the blob, is infinite.

I would invoke a similar mechanism, albeit less drastic, for hypochondriacal disturbances. Here the 'fever', 'tumour' or 'infarction' as it were constitutes a narrator-cum-signaller of the constant danger of the barely adequate α-function's being overwhelmed by the arrival of emotional fevers, agglomerations of β-elements (betalomas) or emotional blows. It is as if there constantly existed another scene with *Jurassic Park*-type proto-emotions that periodically threaten to burst into day-to-day reality:[6] in this case, thermometers, medical analyses, X-rays and tests of various kinds are 'merely' (although that is not insignificant) an inquiry into the proximity and dangerousness of this other emotional scene, whose sudden irruption on to the stage of everyday life was feared.

Similar considerations could be applied to obsessional syndromes, in which the pillars of the dam are reinforced and the looming masses of 'undigested facts' are kept under constant control; or to phobic pathologies, in which the 'undigested facts' are agglomerated and ultimately contained through the non-negotiability of the 'phobic lump', which is tantamount to a culture of β-elements.

All pathologies could thus be redescribed on the basis of this model of the mind. Useful as the model is as an aid to establishing the origin of the disturbance, it is particularly valuable in that it lends itself to being immediately placed within a relational system in the analysis, which becomes the locus of the first-time occurrence of unprecedented mental facts. These constitute the initial big-bang represented by the kindling of mental life, which can occur only if there is a relationship with another mind, thus triggering the relevant mechanism: instead of being evacuated, β-elements are taken in and returned transformed into α-elements – in particular enriched with quanta of 'alphaness' that will subsequently permit the kindling of an autonomous α-function (Bion 1962).

The aim will therefore be to set this sequentiality of primordial psychic events in motion. In more favourable cases, on the other hand, it will be a matter of conferring 'digestibility' on the undigested facts that have accumulated over time in the form of quantities of β-elements that have not attained transformability and been transformed into α-elements (Gaburri and Ferro 1988).

For these events to occur, the 'disease' borne by the patient must *infect the field*: the field must to some extent contract the very disease from which the patient is suffering, which thus becomes a disease of the field, and the field must then be transformed by itself undergoing a healing process. Once this has taken place, the healing can be introjected by the patient into his internal world and reaccommodated in his history – which will in a way be a new history, along the lines illustrated in Figure 1.

All this is possible only by way of narrations – the ongoing narrative transformations that constitute the fabric of the analytic field.

A patient says: 'I've got a terrible sore throat; the doctor tells me it's an old deep wound in a tonsil and it's full of pus again. It hurts and I can't swallow.' If this patient is at an advanced stage of analysis and *his α-function is in perfect order*, we might – perhaps – use one of our interpretative codes and suggest a 'different' reading of his communication: there is something – an old wound that has been reopened – that he thought was healed but is hurting again, so he is talking about some emotional suffering, although he has chosen a bodily register in which to narrate it to us.

However, if the patient is only just beginning his analysis, or *a fortiori* if his α-function, or his apparatus for thinking thoughts (Ps ↔ D; ♀♂) is not fully operational, then I believe we must try a different approach. *We* must enter into his world of tonsils, old wounds and pus, using his *narremes* to make the β-elements of the field less toxic, and thus provide him with quanta of alphaness

Figure 1 Scene from a Corto Maltese story [Translator's note: Corto Maltese is the sailor and adventurer hero of novels, comics and cartoons by the Italian writer Hugo Pratt (1927–95)]

that he can introject. Here, the first interpretation mentioned above, although 'true' (in terms of a psychoanalytic code of our own), would constitute –K because it would arise from our mind only (Riolo 1989); it would be a persecutory primal scene, because we should in effect be engaged in coitus with a theory of our own and ultimately – partly through the activation of jealousy and envy – be overtaxing not only his apparatus for thinking thoughts but also his inadequate α-function.

We should be doing what a patient of mine told me after I had given him an excessively saturated and exhaustive interpretation: he responded by mentioning a scene from Wim Wenders' 1987 film *Der Himmel über Berlin*, in which the angels took the essence of a feather, leaving the weight of materiality to people. Although we must not be anorexic angels who leave the 'materiality' and its weight with the patient, we must be able to let ourselves be contaminated with the 'material' of their narrations and to go where it takes us. Eventually we shall be able to teach the patient to conceive of the mind in thought, by way of all the signals conveyed to us in a thousand dialects by the mind about itself and its functioning and dysfunctioning (de León de Bernardi 1988, 1991).

However, you cannot teach a child to ride a bicycle by showing him a video of a winning sprint by Fausto Coppi.[7] You have to be there, behind him, holding him, making sure he keeps his balance, watching out for potholes and stones, and helping him if he falls, until he learns to maintain his 'own' equilibrium.

Again, if the field fails to contract the patient's disease, anything not expressed in a disease of the field cannot be treated and will stay like the patient's 'undigested fact'. Having said that, however, I believe there is always a gradient of impermeability of the field that is directly proportional to the unanalysed or unanalysable residues.

Another by no means negligible problem is the analyst's possible phobia about 'contracting a disease', which is also a constituent of the field. He will use this phobia as a criterion of analysability, and will thus exclude patients whose illness he does not wish to be infected by. This may also apply to certain aspects of the patients he does accept for analysis: for instance, he may be happy to work with the neurotic parts but not with the psychotic or, *a fortiori*, the autistic parts.

Another question again arises here: are there times when it is necessary to impose a strong, radical interpretative caesura, negating the patient's manifest communication and revealing a profoundly different sense? I sometimes find myself doing this, and then it often becomes an engine of the analysis, because, even if the patient responds with rage or frustration, that imparts motion to the field. As Bleger (1966) writes, breaches of the setting by the analyst may ultimately be useful and inevitable, but can by no means be perpetrated on purpose.

However, this in my view is a function of the analyst's own emotional needs: I like to think of the analyst as a Michelangelo, with his powerful technique of the unfinished, and as a great storyteller, who knows how to bring to life narremes and stories of the patient and of the field, and is free to detach himself from his psychoanalytic knowledge in order to sail beyond the Pillars of Hercules, beyond the psychoanalytically known, towards new worlds of unthought thinkability and the thoughts in search of a thinker that await us in the Americas of the mind.

The analyst's narcissism and interpretation

At the 1977 EPF [European Psychoanalytical Federation] Congress in Estoril, Eric Brenman presented a fine paper (Brenman 1977) on the narcissism of the analyst, in which he clearly illustrates the various forms in which the analyst's narcissism can interfere with the analytic work, as well as the various ways in which the patient signals such interference.

My own approach to this subject is to consider whether the analyst perhaps assumes a narcissistic position whenever he sets himself up strongly and univocally as the *interpreter* of what is happening *to* the patient. This vision of a 'strong interpreter' of another's truth is already to some extent diluted in the field conceptualizations of Willy and Madeleine Baranger (Baranger, W. 1960; Baranger, M.

and Baranger, W. 1961–2, 1964, 1969; Baranger, M. et al. 1983, 1988; Baranger, M. 1992; Baranger, W. et al. 1994). Here the analyst, using his 'second look' while admittedly acting as an interpreter, interprets only what happens to the analytic 'couple' whenever a 'crossed' resistance (a bulwark) forms.

Moreover, in my view, even in a field context (in which the excessive asymmetry between analyst and patient is already diluted), 'strong and univocal' interpretative activity by the analyst may constitute anti-knowledge (–K), which thus belongs in Column 2 of Bion's Grid.

An analyst whose approach is to 'decode' the patient's text is like the boy I have mentioned in an earlier contribution (Ferro 1992), who responded to a transference interpretation of mine that prematurely saturated the sense by saying: 'I saw some scientists on TV slicing up an egg to see what it was like inside: what a pity, because that stopped the chick from hatching.' The analyst ought to adopt a similar approach to that of Alda Merini in *Sogno e poesia* ['Dreams and poetry'], in which the meaning of pictures is brought out by a poem.[8]

Yet the analytic situation *necessarily involves a degree of asymmetry*, because the analyst is *responsible for the progress of the analysis and for the therapy*, as Di Chiara (1979) points out in his exemplary article on the analytic status of patients.

Taking a broader view

At this point a digression on interpretation is called for. The theme of interpretation in psychoanalysis (Freud 1924, 1937; Etchegoyen 1986, 1996; Eizirik 1993, 1996; Kernberg 1993, 1996; Ferro 1995a) is necessarily bound up with that of interpretation in narratology, of which it must indeed be seen as a sub-theme, albeit with characteristics all of its own (Eco 1962; Eco et al. 1992).

Moreover, 'interpretation' was not invented by twentieth-century literary studies theorists: its origins in western thought date back to the medieval disputes over the meaning of the Word of God (Collini 1995).

However, in more recent times, interest has centred on the nature of sense and the possibilities and limits of interpretation (Eco 1990), in a gradient that directs attention to the role of the reader in the process of the production of sense, and reaching its extreme form in the theses of the deconstructionists (De Man 1971, 1986; Derrida 1977; Miller 1980; Culler 1982; Arrigoni and Barbieri 1998), which allow the reader to produce 'drifts' with increasing levels of meaning, extending even to the point of uncontrolled and unlimited readings.

In this approach with its infinitely divergent possibilities, a fundamentally important position is adopted by Eco (1990) with regard to the 'limit' of possible interpretations: by emphasizing that certain readings are 'overinterpretations', he is raising the problem of the dialectic between the rights of the texts and those of their interpreters. Eco also holds that, if it is claimed that a text has virtually no limits, this does not mean that every interpretative act can have a happy existence: in his view, between the author's intention and that sought by the interpreter, there exists the *intention of the text*. The criteria for ascertaining this original intention of the text are stated to be as follows: (a) coherence (identification of the topic, allowing the relevant isotopies to be established), and (b) economy (the interpreter should not go too far in astonishment and wonder by pursuing details that cannot be assembled into a unitary whole).

However, let us return to the specificity of interpretation in psychoanalysis. It is characteristic of psychoanalytic interpretation that it enters into a relationship and co-determines a text subject to ongoing transformation, in accordance with the interpreter's approach. Yet this has not always been so: the structural approach (Arlow 1985) postulates the existence of neutrality on the part of an interpreter-analyst, whose task is to reveal a text that already exists and has been lost, as in the archaeological metaphor, even if a 'living archaeology' (Green 1973) is involved.

Yet even an approach directed more to the patient's internal objects ultimately leads to a belief in the possibility of a neutral reading of the patient's internal reality and – precisely – of his internal objects and fantasies.

The notion of co-construction and co-determination of what comes to life in analysis arose only with the introduction of field theories. Already in the thought of the Barangers, and to an even greater extent following that of Corrao (1986, 1987, 1992), Bezoari and Ferro (1990a, 1990b, 1991a, 1991b, 1992a, 1992b) and Ferro (1992, 1996a), as well as, I would say, in the entire field-derived Italian school, the text is actually a function of the present interaction between analyst and patient and of the emotional field, to which analyst and patient impart life within an analytic setting. From this point of view, I regard the field (Baranger and Baranger 1961–2, 1964, 1969; Ferro 1993c, 1994b, 1994d) as the matrix of possible stories.

Here, there is a continuous oscillation between the 'negative capability' of the analyst (Bion 1970), i.e. his capacity to remain in doubt, in Ps (a very special Ps, as Bion points out, in that it is devoid of persecution), allowing the opening up of infinite stories (or infinite senses), on the one hand, and, on the other, the choice of the 'selected fact'. That is the strong choice of an interpretative hypothesis which arises from an emotion that aggregates what was dispersed in Ps into a gestalt that closes the possible senses in favour of a prevalent sense, which in turn univocally reorganizes from a given vertex what has formed in the field. This is an operation that takes place in D and entails mourning for that which is not.

This is equivalent to the narratological concepts of an 'open work' and of the 'narcotization' of possible stories in order to allow the development of just one story, as effectively demonstrated by Diderot (1796) in *Jacques the Fatalist* (see Ferro 1992). This book tells 'the story of the love of Jacques for Denise', which the valet, at his master's request, begins to recount on the second page, but never finishes . . . Every time he resumes his account, he is interrupted by an incident or a digression resulting from a request by his master, or else an interlocutor comes on to the scene and speaks in his place. After a meeting with a new female character, the author interrupts the narration and addresses the reader:

> What couldn't this adventure become in my hands, if I took it into my head to tease you! I should make that woman an important character – the niece of the neighboring village curate. I should stir up the peasants of that village; I should prepare all sorts of combats and love affairs, for, actually, this peasant woman was beautiful beneath her petticoats. Jacques and his master had noticed that. Love has not always awaited such an attractive situation. Why couldn't Jacques fall in love a second time? Why couldn't he be a second time the rival, and the preferred rival at that, of his master? – You mean that had already happened once. What? More questions! Don't you want Jacques to get on with his love story? For the last time, make yourself clear: would you like him to, or wouldn't you? If you would, then let's put our peasant girl back on the horse behind her companion, let them go and we'll get back to our two voyagers.
>
> (Diderot 1796: 31f)

In other words, the author is forgoing all the possible stories *in favour of the story that is pressing to be told*, which involves the loss of other narrative possibilities; even so, the novel ends with three possible conclusions, which the reader can choose according to his taste.

That is to say, there must be a constant oscillation between the opening and the closure of sense, as with Ps ↔ D in Bion's theory (Bion 1962, 1963, 1965, 1966, 1975, 1980).

So *Jacques the Fatalist* appears as a navigable channel between the Charybdis of infinite openings of sense and the Scylla of total saturation, predetermination and predictability.

An infinite opening of sense would lead to the situation described by Borges (1941a) in his extraordinary short story 'The garden of forking paths', which cannot fail, at the beginning, to give rise to a loss of bearings and to agoraphobic anxiety at the absence of limits:

> In all fiction, when a man is faced with alternatives he chooses one at the expense of others. In [. . .] Ts'ui Pên, he chooses – simultaneously – all of them. He thus *creates* various futures, various times which start others that will in their turn branch out and bifurcate in other times. [. . .] Fang [. . .] has a secret. A stranger knocks at his door. Fang makes up his mind to kill him. Naturally there are various possible outcomes. Fang can kill the intruder, the intruder can kill Fang, both can be saved, both can die and so on and so on. In Ts'ui Pên's work, all the possible solutions occur, each one being the

> point of departure for other bifurcations [that determine] an infinite series of times, in a dizzily growing, ever spreading network of diverging, converging and parallel times.
>
> (Borges 1941a: 75 and 77)

In certain respects, this story suggests the possibility of *exercises* that we could undertake outside our analytic sessions on Bion's Grid, which remains indefinitely open and usable, in the same way as the exercises of a musician between concerts.

Yet Borges's story 'closes' at a certain point: 'This web of time – the strands of which approach one another, bifurcate, intersect or ignore each other through the centuries – embraces every possibility' (Borges 1941a: 77). Here, we seem to fall into the very mirror image of what the story seemed to be promising – that is, into totally foreseen claustrophobia. This is what Borges, once again quite admirably, offers us in another story, 'The library of Babel'. This is a 'total' library, whose

> shelves contain all the possible combinations of the twenty-odd orthographic symbols [. . .]; that is, everything which can be expressed, in all languages [including] the faithful catalogue of the Library, thousands and thousands of false catalogues, a demonstration of the fallacy of these catalogues, a demonstration of the fallacy of the true catalogue, [. . .] the interpolations of every book in all books.
>
> (Borges 1941b: 61)

This is a perfect description of the claustrophobic, sterile circle of already saturated theories – 'as already propounded by Freud' – or, as it were, of a text that merely awaits decoding in the form of a transliteration, along the lines of a Kleinian unconscious bodily fantasy.

But let us return to the field and the need for it to have 'unpredictable openings' and 'necessary closures' of sense (Bion Talamo 1987; Rocha Barros 1994). From this point of view, the concatenation of 'selected facts' entails the development of the story of the couple in one of its dialects – that of the story, of the internal world, of the relationship or of the field.

The limit of the possible stories (Ferro 1996a) is that they should as far as possible arise from the transference (understood as repetition and the projection of fantasies) and from the patient's emotions (or proto-emotions) or β-elements, and that they should proceed in the direction $\beta \rightarrow \alpha$ and should not therefore serve for confirmation of the analyst's theories.

On the basis of earlier publications of mine, let me now summarize what seem to me to be the particular characteristics of the field according to this conception.

Fluidity of the field

Except when afflicted by serious pathology, the field possesses the characteristic of continuous variation, because it is traversed (and constituted) by emotional lines of force, turbulences and proto-emotions *in statu nascendi* that belong to the couple and are constantly transformed into fluid narrations, with ongoing formation of α-elements. In Cavazzoni's novel *The Voice of the Moon* (1987), on which the Fellini film of the same name is based, a prefect asks a geographer to map his province. Although the geographer tries, the factual reality of the province is constantly changing, so that, after attempting to draw maps, which gradually become easier to update by superimposition, even using tissue paper, he concludes that a 'water atlas' would be appropriate, given the wavering nature of the region's borders, in line with reality. I quote:

> 'And then, if there were currents inside the atlas, the ink of the printing could flow and spread, like clouds when there is wind. And where we've printed words on the water, or colours, to indicate the mountains and the grasslands where the native tribes feed their flocks, and where we've printed shading or cross-hatching to indicate foggy valleys, [. . .] gradually, due to the nature of water, all these words and patterns will dissolve and turn streaky; or they may turn into a rainbow, which would give great pleasure to look at.' [The prefect] could see in his mind's eye the printed lines and letterings swimming in this liquid atlas, and dissolving and coming together again, in such a way as to suggest a geography that changed before your very eyes, and had the visual quality of iridescent cloth.
>
> (Cavazzoni 1987: 156).

So the field coincides with the narration that is made of it (Rocha Barros 1992), which is already out of date at the very moment when it is completed, because new characters and emotional forces are constantly 'in search of an author' (Ferro 1993d) or, as the Barangers put it, there is a continuous oscillation between the constitution of bulwarks and their dissolution through the 'analyst's second look'.

Destructuring of previous configurations

The very moment of constitution of the field coincides with the destructuring of the identities and emotional lines of force of every one of its constituents. The gestalt that takes shape is something absolutely new, which can be described only *a posteriori* (Ferro 1994a). A fine tale by Woody Allen – 'The Kugelmass episode', which I have cited before (Ferro 1992) – tellingly exemplifies the narrative deconstruction of the textual configuration prior to a meeting.

Oscillation between infinite openings of sense and limits in the construction of possible worlds

The field becomes the matrix for the genesis of infinite stories and infinite possible journeys, which take shape in the interaction between its variables (Ferro 1995d, 1995e), always provided that these are transformational events ($\beta \rightarrow \alpha$) and that the transformation arises out of the patient's proto-emotions awaiting thinkability. The limit, then, is that the stories shall not serve for confirmation of the analyst's theories, but for narrative transformation of the β-elements of the field, in a manner consistent with the story and with the patient's internal world.

This can be illustrated by two stories. The first is Maurizio Nichetti's 1993 film *Stefano Quantestorie*,[9] which I have mentioned before (Ferro 1996a), but which I should like to adduce again briefly here. Stefano, the hero, experiences a large number of possible stories of his own existence, according to the prevalent emotional tone of his relationship with his parents. If in a given situation Stefano's mother had been particularly apprehensive, his life would have taken a different turn (which is narrated), and if, on another occasion, the father had been less present, Stefano would have . . . and so on, and so on, to the point where different possible developments of Stefano's life are narrated, all of them stemming from different tonalities in the affective encounter. The limit is that the story is always relevant to the field.

A story in which this is not the case is illustrated in the famous cartoon (Figure 2) that shows Snow White's witch with the poisoned apple in her hand,

Figure 2 Snow White's witch presents herself to Little Red Riding Hood and the Wolf

in front of a doorway in which Little Red Riding Hood and the Wolf are standing; she is told: 'Sorry, madam, you've got the wrong fairy-tale.' This indicates that narrative inconsistency imposes a limitation on the drift into possible worlds. As Baranger et al. (1988: 124) point out, as 'analysts we cannot propose to anyone any history that is not his own'.

Non-saturation

The concept of the field imparts vastly greater breadth to the 'narrow' concept of relationship, enabling us to think of 'emotional facts' or 'proto-emotions' as present 'in the room' before they can be conveyed through the relationship. They can then be regarded as existing in a kind of intermediate area, in which scenes and characters that would otherwise remain confined within the straitjacket of a premature explicit relational formulation can live and take shape. Considered in these terms, relationship is one of the functions of the field.

I recall a patient who responded to a saturated transference interpretation of mine that blocked off the communication by saying: 'I saw some shamans tearing an antelope to pieces with their bare hands to look inside it and read the future; they didn't seem to care that they were killing a living being.'

Transformations

In accordance with developments that take more account of *transformations* in the session, as the ongoing production and construction of sense, than of *interpretations* as instances of decoding of meaning, the field can be conceived not as something that constantly needs to be made explicit in the here and now, but as the 'medium' that permits operations of transformation, as well as subsequent narratives and small insights, which do not require interpretation but presage further changes: it is precisely the field which, in proportion as it is explored, constantly expands (Bion 1970), becoming the matrix of possible stories, many of which are left 'in store' pending the possibility of development.

This entails constant attention to the patient's capacity for taking new insights on board, and not taxing his α-function and 'apparatus for thinking thoughts' (Ps ↔ D; ♀♂) beyond the limit of tolerability – otherwise the result will be only persecution, which will immediately be signalled in the text of the session. The patient is not 'under investigation', and is indeed our 'best colleague' (Bion 1978, 1985, 1997), with whom unforeseeable journeys can be constructed; moreover, even what is not immediately interpreted 'remains' as the warp and weft of the field itself (Robutti 1992a, 1992b).

Characters

The status of the characters of an analytic session differs according to one's model. The gradient extends from characters understood in a historico-referential sense to characters as internal objects, who are thus citizens of the patient's internal world, as well as to characters understood as 'names' that describe a quality of the functioning of the couple in a place in the field (Ferro 1992, 1996a, 1996f; Bezoari and Ferro 1990a, 1991b, 1992b); the whole of Chapter 7 will be devoted to this subject.

The first session after the summer holidays allows us to reflect on the 'apparatus for thinking thoughts' (Bion 1962) and on how communications 'in' the field should be understood. I regard the *first* session after the holiday period as particularly important, not only for the patient's account of how it was experienced, but also, and in particular, for gleaning the 'seeds' that may subsequently sprout in the field.

Returning after the summer holidays, Rosa told me that 'in spite of all the points' she had accumulated, she had not been able to obtain a transfer to Pavia . . . that after a long journey to a place where the 'heather was in flower', she had had the problem of finding a *lettino* for the night,[10] as there were three people in a double room and an additional *lettino* was needed . . . then she told me about the Castellana caves . . . how a friend had died in a motorcycle accident . . . this had been a very painful loss for his wife, who, however, like all widows, would eventually come to terms with it and form other relationships – as well as for the mother, who had looked after her son . . . then she mentioned an arid, emotion-denying character . . . and finally an intense, living relationship with a woman friend and her daughter . . .

In my view, interpretation of these introductions to possible narrations would have prevented them from developing: the seeds are there, but need time to ripen – the theme of 'all the points' and hence of the deep wounds; the theme of something flowering even in a faraway place, like longing; the problem of the *lettino* (as the analytic couch); the theme of depth (the caves); the theme of loss and the various degrees to which it can be worked through; . . . and the theme of the quality of the soil (arid or fertile) . . .

This is illustrated diagrammatically in Figure 3: if S represents the 'white light' of the field, S_1 to S_n are the rays of their spectrum of narration and renarration as refracted through the prism Ps ↔ D / ♀♂ (apparatus for thinking thoughts). That is to say, the separation is renarrated through its constitutive threads.

$S = S_1 + S_2 + S_3 + \ldots S_n$ represents the function of the apparatus for thinking thoughts; this must be radically distinguished from the image-generating α-function, which has worked well in this case, yielding appropriate images.

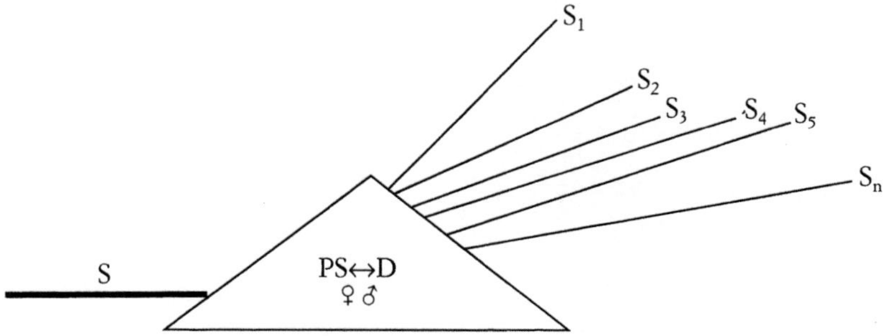

Figure 3 Narratability spectrum of an emotional experience

2

Telling ourselves stories with, perhaps, a grain of truth

The following clinical examples demonstrate how a shared narration takes shape in the session – a narration that necessarily draws on the emotional genomes of patient and analyst, and is therefore the legitimate child of both. The whole of this chapter is thus a narration of the previous chapter in the form of images.

Marcella

The functioning of this young analysand, a brilliant mathematician, has for a long time been flat and two-dimensional; her desk is full of long strings of theorems and equations which she uses to construct a defensive barrier against any kind of contact. My immediate fantasy is of being in the presence of one of those big cephalopods that squirt out jets of ink when they sense danger. Any attempt at a closer approach or at interpretation, however cautious, merely intensifies the 'ink jets'. I feel that patience is all I can rely on.

My caution pays off: little by little, there appear on the 'desktop' not only what Marcella calls 'official' relationships but also affective ones.

In a session in which I am able to help bring about the creation of a *good, non-persecutory climate*, 'infantile memories' begin to appear, including one in which – she does not know if she actually recalls this or if it was told to her by her mother – using a baby-walker she was moving along a corridor on to which three rooms opened (Marcella, of course, has three sessions per week); she went faster and faster until eventually she bumped violently into the basin in the bathroom at the end of the corridor. The session ends in this way, leaving me pleased at the emergence of this deeper, more personal level.

During the ten minutes which I allow between patients in my usual setting,[1] I become aware of a sudden, intense headache. I wonder why this is happening, because it is very unusual for me. I worry about the next session: how will I be able to work with the 'new patient'?

I sense that it has something to do with Marcella – and at this point I understand *my headache*, the concern about the next session and the 'new patient'. A change has occurred, connected not with an identification of mine with the patient, but with the budding, somewhere in the field, of a powerful emotion, or rather of an attack of mental pain or psychic suffering which confirms that a leap in mental growth is at hand. All that can be seen of it at this stage is its precursor in the field – but once something comes alive in the field, it is not long before it can also be taken stably on board by the patient.

What do I mean by my helping to bring about a good climate, as mentioned above? Is it a spurious acquiescence on the part of the analyst, or a pretence that nothing is afoot? By no means; nor does it have anything to do with the careful dosing of the temperature and distance of interpretations (Meltzer 1976). It is in my view essential to respect the patient's threshold of tolerability, or rather that of his apparatus for thinking thoughts, or indeed of his apparatus for generating thoughts (the α-function), on the assumption that persecution feelings in the session are substantially a signal of excessive stress: the α-function, ♀♂ and Ps ↔ D emit a *signal* when they are overtaxed. If this signal goes unheeded, 'thoughts' (or β-elements) are evacuated as β-elements, giving rise to 'waking-dream snapshots', to acting out, to basic assumption behaviour and to psychosomatic manifestations in the patient's body or in that of the setting (arriving late for sessions, or skipping them altogether). In the session reported here, the 'pain' appears as a response to the 'stoppage' represented by the weekend and to the 'stoppage' resulting from my telling the patient the dates of the summer holidays.

A few sessions later, Marcella arrives about a quarter of an hour late; this is very unusual for her, even though she comes from another town. She tells me that she is late because the train *inspector* saw a drug addict getting into a carriage and locking himself in the toilet, and did his best to persuade him to get off the train. He succeeded, but then the boy got back on to the train, and the inspector had to have all the train's doors locked so as to get him off again. The whole episode lasted, precisely, a quarter of an hour.

I could easily give an academic interpretation ('a part of you acted as an inspector to make sure you did not get to the session . . . because you feel you need analysis so badly . . .'), but I feel that it would be too one-sidedly mine (–K!),[2] and that it would not be accepted by the patient and produce insight, but might cause only persecution and loss of contact.

I make neutral comments about this situation. When I ask how it felt to her, my question triggers an account of some 'childhood memories' about her father's job as a *railwayman*[3] . . . she recalls a whole family vocabulary, as well as the fact that railwaymen have to pay for any delays for which they are responsible . . . that serious difficulties arise if someone *tries to commit suicide by jumping under a train* . . . and goes on to discuss the occupational risks facing other workers, like a physiotherapist friend of hers who was violently attacked by a patient. The narration continues, until I ask: 'Might there be any connection between these dramatic stories – suicides, attempted murders, the drug addict – and my telling you the holiday dates last time?'

Marcella laughs in relief and (to my surprise) says: 'If we don't have just an official relationship any more, but also an emotional one . . . well, then some of the emotions are violent, and they can't always be controlled by the inspector . . .'

'So,' I comment, 'the inspector might as well not have caused this delay by trying to hold back the mixture of despair and rage that you call the drug addict.'

I make no distinction between the different forms of a patient's communications – dreams, narrations, childhood memories, anecdotes, etc. – but merely try to make contact with the α-element, the narrative sequence of α-elements, or the narrative derivatives of the α-element. The patient constantly selects narrative derivatives of α-elements for us, in order to assign meaning for us to the field's emotional pictogram, or its emotional pictographic chain. An α-element is simply the pictographed synthesis of the resultant of the patient's emotional–relational situation, in a given space–time of the field. It is like the Giorgio Forattini cartoon featured on the front page of the Italian newspaper *La Repubblica*. Constantly and frame by frame, the patient films his own exteroceptions, proprioceptions and proto-emotions, and stores them as α-elements. Of these, we may perceive only the narrative derivatives, except in a few rare cases of waking-dream flashes, which are projected and seen externally.

Patients' narrations stem from their α-elements, and are for us perceptual-emotional afferences that activate, or ought to activate, α-elements, as the fruit of reverie, or less sophisticated elaborations if they already reach us in the form of thoughts that will either commit us to the 'selected fact' or engage our attention in terms of their composition and structure (♀♂ and Ps ↔ D). Similarly, a 'childhood memory' is merely a syncretic account (the narrative derivative of the α-element) whose sense is clarified in relation to the present, even if it is not necessarily made explicit as such.

Stefania

My first sight of the patient is impressive. I open the door in a dismal mood, of the kind that often assails me on a foggy Saturday morning at nine, and am confronted with a gorgeous young woman with a vertiginously plunging neckline and carrying an enormous suitcase. I need not dwell on the fantasies inspired by this vision, which lights up the gloom of that April morning. She sits down and tells me that she has come because of an interview with me on 'infantile seductions and the memory of them' that she read in *L'Unità*.[4] She has a tormenting memory of an episode in her childhood when, at the age of 10, she went for a catechism lesson for her communion and the sacristan tried to put his hands inside her blouse. I am struck by the coincidence with my own instant fantasies, and try to widen the conversation to her suitcase and all the things she must be carrying around with her.

She tells me a long story of a difficult adolescence, with a remote mother and father, who were separated and in conflict with each other . . . and goes on to say that she would like to have a relationship of 'deep spiritual communion' with her boyfriend, whereas all he can think of is sex.

So the 'childhood memory' is nothing other than a snapshot of Stefania's current problem: how to reconcile her need for tenderness and intense emotional closeness (communion) with an explosive sensuality that she has not been able to integrate. She has come to me with a view to unifying these aspects (*L'Unità* – i.e. unity). Here we have a particularly successful oneiric cartoon (α-elements) featured on the front page as a token of the unresolved subject-matter – the undigested fact – that calls for a narrative transformation to allow new developments.

Marina

Marina is a girl who suffers from panic attacks, but is now otherwise quite well integrated. On arriving for her session, she tells me that she has finally realized that she is on another planet, inhabited by metal androids, and that her own mother is a robot. I am overcome with fear bordering on panic; I think she must have had a psychotic breakdown and that I must find a colleague to give her the tranquillizer Serenase.[5] Then I stop to think what could have happened. I run my mind back over the recent period. I had told Marina that we would have to change next week's Friday session to Thursday. I know that this puts her out very much, because for her the sessions are like Tom Thumb's pebbles, but I also remember that last week we were able for the first time to miss out a session altogether without rescheduling it.

She had had some dreams: a little girl was left by herself in a house in the mountains, and it wasn't clear if she had enough food and firewood; there was a woman who was widowed, but then news arrived that her husband was perhaps not dead after all. These dreams had helped us to fill the gap left by the missed session and to understand the emotions activated.

In another dream, she had run trustingly to her father who was waiting for her on the other side of a little bridge . . . but then I had been ill and had to cancel the next two sessions, so the meeting had not happened.

She had coped with all this . . . but the new communication about the rescheduled session had been the last straw . . . it had made her feel as if she was in a weird world with affectless *metal people* . . .

I tell her all this in simple terms, going back over the story of the last two weeks. She responds with relief, telling me a dream in which a mad surgeon was transplanting kidneys instead of hearts . . . and so on . . . just as I was doing with the sessions . . .

The possibility of a transformational narration and of selected facts, appropriately linked together, banishes from the scene the persecution which the α-function was now scarcely able to represent by a 'tranquil' pictograph;[6] hence my fantasy of the tranquillizer – something to lighten the burden on the α-function and the apparatus for thinking thoughts.

On another occasion when one of Marina's sessions has to be rescheduled, she dreams that her own father, a cardiologist, is very ill; the ward sister, to whom she gives a prescription to help her father, but who takes no notice of it, says that 'the little bears are fine . . . it's nice to go on holiday' . . . I interpret the dream as being about the patient's separation anxieties . . . on hearing the telephone ring in the room next door, she thinks it is a woman patient she saw arriving, who was in tears and seemed to her to be desperate. Then she recalls a TV movie, *Gamma*, in which someone was performing a brain transplant (installing cassettes to recondition the new brain with the right memories), but a criminal switched the cassettes and turned the patient into a killer. Then she tells me about a woman friend of hers who is always furious, and goes around with a knife in her bag.

If I fail to realize the crisis that afflicts me, like the cardiologist father, whenever the setting is modified, and I interpret in Column 2 instead of picking up the most immediate anxieties, and if I am not prepared to look into her prescription, the climate gets worse and worse, ultimately inducing fury on her part and again dehumanizing the analysis, while the pain is split off into 'the patient she saw arriving'.

There is always a great temptation for the analyst to operate in Column 2 (the column of lies). In this case it was simpler for me to interpret the anxiety as being connected with the holidays, for which I was basically not so responsible, than to accept the burden of the patient's ill-being as due to my breach of the setting. Bion in fact draws attention to this risk repeatedly – most clearly in the Italian seminars (Bion 1985).

Martina

For a long time Martina has been afraid of 'being a vegetable'. After a few months of analysis, she dreams of a heart-shaped 'big red radish', and then of a little bird's heart developing and beating.

Certain narrations can sometimes be construed in a relational sense: if my interpretation touches her too closely, there appears 'Tinto Brass',[7] or, on occasion, 'barbecued meat' on an iron grill (F).[8]

But all of a sudden, just before the holidays, an emotional field with a large number of focal points is activated, and has to be respected over a long period, in the *fabulae* it brings to life. The *first* concerns a couple separating owing to a crisis of jealousy . . . with mutual rage and ill-feeling . . . with affective dissatisfaction in one partner and sexual dissatisfaction in the other. The *second* is the drama of a little girl who constantly hears her parents telling each other that they are not going to live together any more. The *third* is about her falling in love with a workmate and waiting for him trustingly until the holidays are over. Minimal interpretative hints are tolerable, but the field must remain the custodian of other interpretations.

Rosa

Rosa, now at an advanced stage of her analysis, dreams of a studious little man aged about 50, to whom she feels attracted: although he is with a woman, she wants to seduce him and succeeds in making love to him.

I do not know how to take the dream; certain possibilities that I feel to be academic occur to me, and I say only that it seems to me that she is not holding back on her wish to seduce somebody, contrary to her long-held theory that she herself has always been the victim of seductions.

In the next session, she tells me she felt disturbed because Judge Salamone acquitted a little girl's father accused of having seduced his daughter. Then she is anxious at having conceived her second child while the first, a girl of 6, was present in the bedroom, albeit sleeping peacefully. This too seems to her to be a perversion – a successful seduction of her husband. At this point I am bound to remind her that for a long time she was afraid that she had seduced me, on account of the way I looked at her, and her interpretation of my supposed sexual fantasies about her, and that, when she was small, she had thought her father harboured seductive intentions towards her . . .

Now, after the dream and my intervention, the judge's verdict is clear: the father had not been the seducer, but it was *she* who had wanted to seduce the father (forgetting the woman) and myself (forgetting the analysis). Moreover, this fear of seduction also entered into the fear that the decision – shared with me – to terminate the analysis (the second daughter) was the result of a successful seduction of myself, which had taken place in the presence of the first daughter, the now 6-year-old analysis.

She is astonished to realize that she really did think this.

In my view, the chapters of *Elements of Psycho-Analysis* (1963) in which Bion considers in depth the vicissitudes of ♀♂ and Ps ↔ D deserve particularly close attention, together with the fine pages of *Learning from Experience* (Bion 1962) on the development of ♀, ♂ and ♀♂.

It is once again Rosa who brings a dream in which she wanted to make love to an old boyfriend who had abandoned her, but this would have ruined her present happiness, even though it might have helped her to overcome her anxiety at the abandonment. This follows the account of a difficult weekend with her little girl, who had fits of jealousy and excitement about her expected new little sister. The excitement of making love to the old boyfriend is felt to be a corrective to the abandonment.

Then she mentions a little girl who told her therapist that her father had touched her 'twinkie' and a supervisor who had said that glue spilt from the tin might be a reference to her father's semen.

I notice that I have lately been excitedly giving transference interpretations, and suggest to her that there is precisely an excitement – it is immaterial whether it stems from her and is then activated in myself, or whether I am its source, and I then discharge it – that acts as a corrective to the forthcoming mourning for the termination, which is feared as an abandonment, and to the associated feelings of jealousy.

The fur coat and the sandals

Luisa is a patient who envelops me in a blanket of words, which smother me and prevent me from identifying any meaningful thread, however fine, in what she tells me. I could of course interpret all this jabbering as a protective smoke screen, as this seems fairly clear to me, but I decide to wait because I feel that she would not have a place for this interpretation.

She then unexpectedly brings a dream: she was wearing a long, heavy fur coat that completely covered her, but with sandals that left her feet and ankles bare. She then associates to a woman friend's dream in which the friend was afraid because a light suddenly appeared in a dark wood and she was terrified of being attacked. I could easily give an exhaustive interpretation: the patient is signalling that although she covers herself all over with a thick layer of words, something is beginning to show through, as in the dream itself – but suddenly she is afraid of giving away her position, of being discovered, and of being attacked by gunshot-interpretations. I say: 'The dreams are telling us something about covering and uncovering oneself:[9] so what are the dangers to be uncovered?' She answers: 'Well, it's like when I was a teenager: I was accosted by one of those randy old men, who made an obscene suggestion to me, and didn't let me experience my wish for adolescence and discovery.'

If the analyst gives excessively direct, saturated interpretations, he is experienced by the patient as being full of uncontainable sexual/relational desires; he must therefore forgo such interpretations and leave the patient enough time to acquire trust and to discover herself, by doing his best to establish an emotional climate appropriate to discovery. One is inevitably reminded of Winnicott's (1971) comment about the amount of deep change he prevented by his personal need to interpret, and how he later came to enjoy facilitating the patient's creativity more than the sense of having been clever in his interpretations.

In the iguana's belly

For two of Giovanna's sessions, I am more silent and rather less present than usual, because I am still feeling disturbed by the violent psychotic transference of the previous patient.

In the third session, Giovanna brings three dreams. In the first, she was ticked off by a woman friend for being indifferent to everything; in the second, her boyfriend told her that he was going away for six or seven years and a television set was broken and not showing programmes any more; while in the third, she was eaten up by a huge iguana, and although she was protected in its belly, she was also shut in and could not get out until 'it opened its mouth'. She associates to Pinocchio, who, when he and his father are swallowed by a whale, manages to escape by lighting a fire inside its belly.

Together we are able to develop the idea that if she feels that I am less present, she is swallowed up by indifference. It is as if her boyfriend were to go away and leave her alone: the programme is interrupted and she is protected – but she is also a prisoner, imprisoned by indifference inside the cold-blooded iguana, until I start talking again and impart to the relationship the fiery heat that will enable her to emerge from the whale's belly.

The organless little girl

Manuela dreams of a little girl with no liver, no heart and perhaps no other organs either. 'How are we to take this dream?' asks the patient, whose analysis is at an advanced stage. Who will take on this little girl? Is the analyst the one who is 'heartless' and 'lacking in courage' (because he is going on holiday and has suggested an adjustment to her session times to make his schedule more convenient), or is it the patient, who will lack the organs needed to survive if she is without her analysis? But, she adds, the little girl in the dream is in a sort of scientific analytical laboratory, and there's no one there . . . no parents . . . no doctors . . . and no nurses. Well then, could it be the lack of these maternal or paternal 'functions', of a heart, that deprives the little girl of the corresponding organs? This hypothesis excites Manuela.

Carlo's wild goat

On beginning to get back in touch with his manhood and autonomy, Carlo has the following dream: he is in an operating theatre where a wild goat has been anaesthetized for brain surgery . . . the operation is in progress . . . but then the anaesthetic wears off. Instead of interpreting that 'the wild goat is the part which . . .', I ask what happened to the goat. It had to be anaesthetized because there was no grass . . . only ice . . . That was the only way it could survive . . . hunger had driven it mad . . . hence the operation . . .

The gardeners and the danger of fire

A little boy's parents ask me for advice. In the first two interviews, I fail to understand anything: there do not seem to be any particular problems either with the boy or with them. Yet they are worried. I cannot see what is worrying them. Gradually, metaphors of raising emerge – for instance, 'gardeners looking after young plants' . . . The mother then tells me that her 'husband has a brother who flares up like a match' . . . then they suddenly 'catch fire' in front of me over some utterly trivial problem . . . they quarrel . . . they get heated . . . they are quite inflamed . . . and – finally – at the third interview, I become aware of their fear of gardeners, however solicitous they may be, in case the pyromaniac 'brothers' . . . set fire to what they are lovingly caring for. It is now necessary to clarify the problem in terms of their concerns – to inform them of the need for 'foresters' who are aware of this incendiary tendency, which, after all, is indicative of passion and love, but which sometimes risks burning what they love most.

It is in my view absolutely inevitable that the analyst will 'soil' the field with his mental presence (it could not be otherwise); that is the only way to effect the vital graft that will allow genuine creative mingling of the analyst's and patient's emotional genomes, thus breaking the suffocating vicious circle of the compulsion to repeat.

A short story by Arthur Schnitzler, 'Reichtum' ['Riches'], in my view tellingly illustrates this situation.

Schnitzler's 'Riches'

The title of this story could equally well be 'Remembering and repeating without ever working through' (Ferro 1995b). Its hero, a failed artist who ekes out a living as a house-painter, rises one morning and finds himself smartly dressed in tails. Herr Weldein, as he is called, gradually *remembers* what happened to him the night before. Having gambled and won at a tavern, he had been joined by some dissolute noblemen who, for amusement, had dressed him in their smart clothes and taken him to a gambling club, where he won a fortune. But now, as he wakes, where is the money? He *remembers* having been afraid that they might take it away from him, so he did not take it home; he *remembers* certain small clues . . . others emerge tortuously in the next few days . . . he *remembers* bending down . . . he *remembers* the sound of water . . . so he combs the entire town trying to find what he so carefully hid.

To no avail. He despairs for his family, who must go on living in poverty, and for his son Franz: 'Poor Franz, my poor little boy.'

The years go by. Franz has meanwhile become a well-known painter, although the only subjects he can portray successfully are gamblers and gambling dens.

On his deathbed, Weldein suddenly remembers where he hid his treasure, and informs his son of its location. Incredulous, the son goes to the river bank, beside a bridge, where he follows his father's instructions and finds the treasure.

The son looks forward to a life of luxury and riches. But he has a painting to finish. It depicts a gambling hall with gamblers, but seems to him to be *lacking in passion*, so he decides to get someone to take him to the club – the one where his father won the money – to experience the intoxication of gambling, so that he can portray it in his picture. Of course, he loses every penny at the gaming table.

So he goes back to the river bank, digs, fills his pockets with stones and earth, and tells himself that these are his father's fortune. But this does not work: it is not long before he realizes that his pockets are full of stones. At this point his face becomes contorted, virtually assuming the physical features of his father, and he says: 'The money, where did I hide the money . . . ?' Now totally identified with the father when *he* was unable to find the treasure, he says: 'Poor Franz, my poor little boy.'

Let me add that in the background there is a character, *a nobleman*, who could have contributed, in the story both of the father (he was one of the nobles who took him to the gambling club) and of the son (it was he who commissioned the picture from him), to a different outcome: although he could have *transformed the story*, he always merely 'looked on', adopting a neutral, distant stance.

It is of course impossible to overlook the parallel with the 'position of the analyst in the session' (Luzés 1995), who may get involved or remain aloof, watching, but not interacting with, the patient's need for passion and the accumulation of transgenerational fantasies which, if not transformed, will make for an eternal compulsion to repeat (Faimberg 1988).

3

In praise of Row C: psychoanalysis as a particular form of literature

Let me begin this chapter with a brief note on α-elements and their derivatives, so that we can gradually move on from Row B of Bion's Grid (the formation of α-elements) to Row C, in which they are placed in sequence, and to the formation of *narrative derivatives*.

To obviate any misunderstanding of the basic structure of my theoretical and clinical model, I shall outline it again in slightly different terms in the chapters on sexuality and on waking dream thought. Despite the risk of repetition, I hope that this will make for greater clarity.

Bion (1962) postulates that the activity of metabolization which we apply to every perceptual afference is of central importance. This activity consists in the formation, from afferences, of a pictogram, or visual ideogram, which is a poetic image that syncretizes the emotional resultant of the relevant afference or set of afferences – namely, the α-element. These α-elements are not directly accessible in waking life except through the phenomena of 'reverie' and 'oneiric flashes'. They are the way in which every sensory, exteroceptive and proprioceptive experience is pictographed in real time. Each emotional-sensory pictogram is thus placed in a sequence with other α-elements. The sequence of α-elements is unknowable except through their narrative derivatives.

The analyst interprets. The manner in which the patient 'hears' his interpretation is pictographed in an α-element and in a sequence of α-elements. These α-elements are not directly accessible, but are rendered to some extent knowable by their 'narrative derivatives' – that is, by what the patient says immediately after the interpretation. While the patient's words draw on his history and internal world, they surely also draw on what the mind is pictographing at every relational instant.

The 'narrative derivative' is like a literary genre. That is to say, it is independent of the quality and seriation of α-elements. One and the same sequence of α-elements can be narrated by, for example, a childhood memory; an account of 'external' life; a report of a film; a diaristic genre; an intimate-type genre; or an infinite number of other possible modes. However, they all signify the same experience of a sequence of α-elements.

If an interpretation has resulted in the pictographing of α-elements that have to do with pain, violence or oppression, the narrative derivative might be 'I remember once, when I was small, how my father gave me a very painful injection, and then humiliated me in front of everybody because I cried' or 'I saw a film on television in which a girl was assaulted and raped by a hitch-hiker she had given a lift to' or 'Something very unpleasant happened to my aunt the other day: some immigrants tried to mug her because she wouldn't give them what they wanted' or 'A friend of mine came to me in tears because her husband forces her to have violent sex with him with absolutely no tenderness' or 'I dreamt of a Greek god who was pursuing me with spears and wanted to run me through.'

However, what determines the *choice of narrative genre*? In my view, the choice aims to achieve a maximum of correspondence between the α-element and what the subject wishes to express: on each occasion, the 'fact', 'memory', 'story', 'dream' or 'anecdote' most suitable for narrating the particular sequence of α-elements is selected, chosen and 'broadcast'. Moreover, each mind will have its own preference for a particular genre, which it uses because it is most suitable for the purpose.

I include dreams in my enumeration because a dream, when brought in a session, is an event of the relational instant in which it is narrated, while in turn being a narrative derivative of other α-sequences at the time of its narration (this is not so at the time of dreaming).

These 'narrative derivatives' thus also constitute continuous 'signals' of the linguistic and emotional text of the session.

From this point of view, the characters of the session can also be seen as 'functional aggregates' that express the resultant of a particular form of oneiric functioning of the couple (Ferro 1992; Bezoari and Ferro 1992a).

The most common 'narrative derivatives' occurring in adult analyses may also be expressed in other forms (in each case as narrations of α-elements) – for instance, play derivatives (e.g. a child analysand's play after an interpretation); graphic derivatives (drawings made in the session); sensory derivatives (e.g. stomach rumbles, sneezes or coughs); motor derivatives (as signs of acting-in as communication); or oneiric derivatives. The oneiric derivatives are of fundamental importance because they indicate what is in my opinion the vital possibility of using dreams to narrate the here and now – that is, as a story that expresses the quality of the α-element 'kindled' at the relevant moment. This applies in particular to the kind of dreams brought by patients *at a certain point* in the session, when they say: 'A dream occurs to me . . .', or to dreams in response to an interpretation. That is why patients should not be trained to tell their dreams;

instead, the analyst should try to encourage their possible emergence at times when they are meaningful.

Ultimately, then, *the α-element is to the narrative derivative as poetry is to the prose of its paraphrase* – or as an original Chinese ideogram is to its graphic derivatives (Figure 4).

Figure 4 shows the following sequence: first, the drawing representing the origin of the relevant character, and then its development in various calligraphic styles: (a) incisions on tortoiseshell, (b) inscription on bronze, (c) small-seal characters, (d) scribe style, (e) standard style and (f) cursive style.

As readers of earlier contributions of mine will know, my interest in narratology stems from the concept of the 'characters of a text'. This notion extends from psychologistic theories of characters, via the theories of the Propp school and of structuralism, to the more recent theories of character construction by way of the intersection of text and reader on the basis of the reading time (Eco 1979), as exemplified by Calvino's novel *If on a Winter's Night a Traveler* (1979) and, to an even greater extent, by Joyce's *Finnegans Wake* (1939). The focus of my interest later shifted to the construction not only of characters but also of the narrative text – in particular, that of the 'analytic session'.

Row C of Bion's Grid (Figure 5) is the row of dreams, myths, narrations with visual characteristics – and, in my view, also of 'poetry'. Here, the sequence of α-elements takes on a compositional structure, whether it relates to a dream, to myth, or to the private myth of the analytic couple or of the patient. It is the row in which the α-element is not isolated, but in harness with other α-elements.

Its main characteristic is the 'sensory' (visual) reference, but from other vertices, it could also refer to an auditory or coenaesthetic sensoriality; it is thus connected with music or dance. For the sake of simplicity, I shall consider only the visual aspect.

Another characteristic is non-saturation – precisely because the visual sense, together with its narrative derivatives, opens the way to an infinite number of possible senses.

Being with the patient in Row C means refraining from operations of interpretative translation, or transliteration from one dialect to another, and instead working constantly in the original and creative area of the encounter, of the joining of the β-element to the α-function, until it is linked up with other α-elements. It is thus the locus of image creation and hence of the contact barrier. Beta-elements – undigested facts – press urgently to enter the field and to be *transformed* there into α-elements and dreams.

Interpretative decoding is a diametrically opposite operation, which at best takes the form of a 'simultaneous translation' into a dialect more consonant with ourselves. In the worst case, however, it is –K (which is an attack on the patient's α-function and on the creativity of the couple's primal scene, at the place and time of the encounter between β and the α-function).

An arrow is speeding towards a man's chest and is about to wound him. The character has two meanings: 'wound' or 'disease', when referring to the effect of the attack with the arrow; or 'swift', where the speed of the arrow is considered.
In modern Chinese, it appears rarely, in expressions such as:

疾病 jí bìng (disease, disease): disease

疾飛猛進 jí fēi měng jìn (swift, flying, violent, moving forward): swift and impetuous

痢疾 lì ji (dysentery, disease): dysentery

疟疾 nüè ji (malaria, disease): malaria

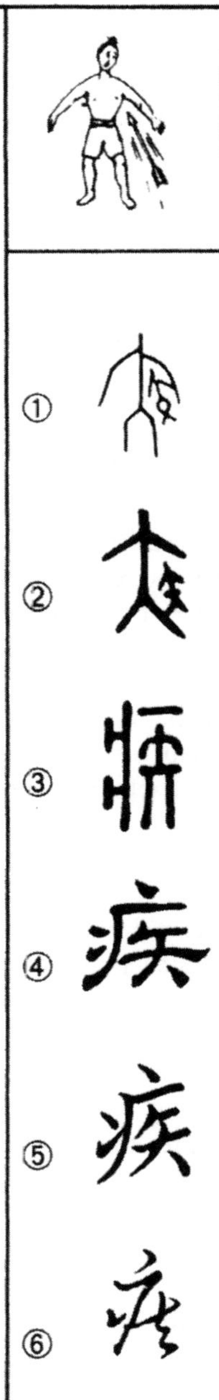

Figure 4 Discussion of a Chinese character [translated from Yuan Huaqing (1998) *La scrittura cinese*, Milan: A Vallardi]

	Definitory hypotheses 1	ψ 2	Notation 3	Attention 4	Inquiry 5	Action 6	...n
A β-elements	A1	A2				A6	
B α-elements	B1	B2	B3	B4	B5	B6	...Bn
C Dream thoughts, dreams, myths	C1	C2	C3	C4	C5	C6	...Cn
D Pre-conception	D1	D2	D3	D4	D5	D6	...Dn
E Conception	E1	E2	E3	E4	E5	E6	...En
F Concept	F1	F2	F3	F4	F5	F6	...Fn
G Scientific deductive system		G2					
H Algebraic calculus							

Figure 5 Bion's Grid

The analyst performs a *narrative transformation* whenever he takes β-elements upon himself and succeeds in giving them an original interpretative construction, in which he confers narrative status on the pressing emotional turbulence or evacuation of β-elements, according to the relevant genre. The analyst, together with the patient, must breathe life into a theatrical scene representing the emotions of the field, thereby opening up increasing and unsaturated levels of sense; as Luzés (1995) puts it, he must impart life to the 'feuilleton'.

In great anger, a very anxious woman patient offers an immediate answer to her own question: 'The boy I saw coming down the stairs as I went up: was he *Qui* [here]?' 'He was not *Qua* [here]!' 'Thank goodness he was not *Quo*!',[1] adds the patient, smiling, thus paving the way for a good start to the session, compared with the extremely bad one that could have ensued.

The visual image resulting from the auditory-to-visual transformation *Qui* → *Qua* revealed the infantile root of the patient's question – namely, a reference to Donald Duck – and the meaninglessness of the question on the adult level: there is no distinction between *Qui*, *Quo* and *Qua*.

That is not all. The patient is also provided with an opportunity for a creative step forward with her reply 'Thank goodness he was not *Quo*!' The result is the creation of a Walt Disney comic strip, which is also the beginning of a fabric of emotions that allow the development of ♀ and is thus a prerequisite for that of ♂. It is in a culture of 'negative capability' that the possibility of a narrative content capable of transforming β arises.

Carlo

After a session I had had to cancel, Carlo arrives for his next session in great anger. He cannot tolerate direct transference interpretations, which literally make him bleed. He at once tells me about something nasty that was done to his son by a spiteful schoolmate, who 'threw his pen [*penna*][2] across the room'. The son made a terrible fuss about the incident, but the patient's wife pooh-poohed it, making the boy cry even more.

My immediate reverie is of a feather being plucked from a chick. With another patient, I feel that I could have used this image, connecting it with the session I had 'plucked out', but I sense that, although this interpretation is the fruit of reverie and supplies an α-element, it would make Carlo bleed. So I must resort to a construction on Row C, diluting the impact of the α-element in a less vivid narrative sequence, and I therefore tell him that his account suggests to me a scene in which a boy happily playing at being an Indian and proud of his feathers has his fun spoilt by a spiteful playmate who has ripped out one of his feathers: one can well imagine that the boy made a fuss about it, as it was after all a nasty thing to do!

After a moment's pause, the patient says:

> But then, you know, my wife put on a cartoon for the boy. Marco calmed down and, that evening, at a party with friends, something happened that I hadn't in the least been expecting: my wife got me dancing in a way that rekindled all my passion for her.

In my view, this narrative function stems from the synergetic operation of the α-function (which creates the emotional pictogram – i.e. the image) and the apparatus for thinking thoughts (♂♀ and Ps ↔ D) (which weaves the narration). I believe, too, that the ultimate aim of analysis is the stabilized introjection of a narrator of this kind, in such a way as to permit emotional transformations from β to α notwithstanding all emotional vicissitudes.

A male patient approaching the end of his analysis had got into the habit, whenever something worried him or made him anxious, of writing an account of the situation, as an extreme way of articulating the cause of the anxiety. This enabled him to make the disturbing element thinkable and then to stand back from what he had written, which he then no longer considered realistic, or to attempt a deeper interpretation of the possible meaning of the original fear.

It will be seen that my conception of the unconscious, as exemplified in this book, differs profoundly from Freud's or Klein's. I subscribe to the idea of the unconscious (due of course to Bion) as an entity downstream of the encounter between β-elements and the α-function, in a state of constant formation and transformation, which calls not for decoding but for ongoing transformation and enrichment, by working on the accumulations of 'undigested facts' (Bion 1962) that are the real promoters of every narration.

I am not concerned here with the capacity of literature to narrate 'psychoanalytic facts' to us in a form often superior to any psychoanalytic theory. In other words, I shall not be considering in depth how literature may lend itself to a categorization of psychoanalytic facts in Row C; after all, the entire subject-matter of psychoanalytic theory finds in Row C a more open, creative and unsaturated form of expression than any other possible exemplification.

However, as stated, that is not the main intention of my approach. My basic vertex is the *need* for the analyst to function in the session as a *co-narrator* so as to allow constant development of the field under investigation.

Narration in the analyst's consulting room

In the *Clinical Seminars*, Bion (1987) states that his response to a patient's communications is to ask himself what story could be told to the patient to facilitate understanding; he adds that the interpretation must be consistent with the patient's capacity for assumption and digestion, as if the patient were a newborn baby. In other words, the need is to find the right way of talking to the patient.

Successful narration

Emilio's architectural barriers

Patrizia is not an easy patient, yet she fits in well with Bion's idea of the patient as 'one's best colleague'. She suffers from panic attacks and I have given her the key to the main entrance of the building where I have my consulting room, for use in 'emergency' only. At the beginning of a session (in which she has finally agreed to lie down on the couch), she insists on being able to open the main entrance door with the key every time. Referring to something that came up in the previous session, I tell her that, whereas on the one hand she is prepared to lie down on the couch, on the other the 'rebellious adolescent' in her wants the keys to the house. Not at all, she says: opening the entrance door helps her to avoid the bad feeling and embarrassment that afflicts her when waiting below and destroys the possibility of a good and constructive session. Then she asks me whether I smoke in sessions with other patients.[3] The question 'demands' an answer; I feel that we are embarking on a session of total incomprehension, which will make her anxious, so that I too will feel disappointed, frustrated and 'fuming' with rage.

I ask myself: 'Suppose I were to try to change this vertex, with its possible elements of decoding and the superego (perhaps –K), and maybe meet her half-way?' I say: 'I think you might be asking me to demolish the architectural barriers that exist between us before we get together.'

It is only after formulating this interpretation that I recall that in the previous session she showed me a photograph of a friend of hers in a wheelchair, who had a brain tumour: in the past, his suffering had horrified and terrified her, but now she could cope with it. So I add that perhaps the demolition of the architectural barriers would allow 'Emilio' (the friend's name) to enter the room, without the bottleneck of waiting or of my silence in response to her questions.

In reply, she says she is afraid that she too might have a brain tumour. This, I tell her, proves that 'Emilio, a paralysed aspect of herself', has really entered the analysis, even if for the time being he needs special arrangements in order to reach us.

Carletto

Carletto comes to his consultation with a box and an exercise book. After a friendly greeting, he takes out some discs ('pogs', which have a picture on the front and a grey back), stacks them up and begins to strike them with other, heavier discs ('slammers'). Whenever a disc turns over, the coloured side is revealed, showing mainly fleas, skulls and a crocodile ('I've got two of these,' he adds). I realize that he is telling me he would like to be helped to lay his cards on the table, revealing them in the same way as he is revealing the pictures on the discs, and it occurs to me that many of my questions might be the slammers, which, on striking the other discs, reveal what is hidden beneath. So I ask him (putting on the same thoughtful air as he seems to be exhibiting): 'Are there lots of things worrying you?' 'Yes, school and my schoolmates.'

'What happens at school?' (Meanwhile he has switched games and is drawing a map of a town, which, he tells me, is Mousetown.) 'The other kids are terrible – especially Albertini, who always thinks people are pinching things from him; he's an absolute bully – and his enemy.'

'He sounds like a Big Bad Pete to me,' I tell him. He smiles at me, and I add: 'And there doesn't seem to be any Chief O'Hara to stop him.' 'That's just how it is,' he answers, and goes on to describe all the evil deeds in which 'Big Bad Pete' would like to involve him, but now he is able to resist – something he could not do when he was small.

I say to him: 'Well, you're a bit like Mickey Mouse, always fighting against Big Bad Pete and his gang.' 'Let me draw you a picture.' With great precision, he then draws a house, a meadow and mountains (Figure 6).

I suddenly have a vision of a landscape seen through the mouth of a crocodile, with teeth in the middle . . . I now imagine Carletto in part fighting with the Big-Bad-Pete-crocodile, from whom he is gradually becoming able to distance himself so that he can enter a world with less greed and less need for appropriation.

I tell him that this landscape, with the meadow and the mountains, is very beautiful. He replies: 'Just imagine: this is the job I want when I grow up . . . working in the woods . . . as a forest ranger . . . feeding the animals and protecting them from poachers.'

At this point I imagine that he has well and truly 'exited' the crocodile's stomach, en route for the new world in which he will be able to take care of his own affects and needs, and to protect them from his internal gang of characteropaths.

Figure 6 A landscape drawn by Carletto

One final comment. Carletto is an adopted child, with problems of unruly behaviour at school and, in the past, of stealing; however, he has become increasingly integrated into the affective reality of his family, through his adoptive parents' loving care. When they originally took him home from the orphanage, he had been diagnosed as autistic. He did not speak, look anyone in the face, or draw pictures. They asked me to monitor him periodically, and to wait for them to be able to take Carletto in before contemplating the possibility of therapy.

The failure of narration and –K

Often the hoped-for transformation fails to materialize, owing either to congestion of narrative capacity by a plethora of emotions that ultimately block the field, or to the emotional unavailability of the analyst (Bolognini 1997). For instance, I notice that when I am tired I tend much more to 'interpret' the patient's communications, instead of being able to play with them in such a way as to bring about transformation. Whereas some patients are relatively tolerant of such an attitude over a long period (or of situations that demand it), others cannot endure anything about them that stems from one mind only (Riolo 1989).

Stefano

Working with Stefano at such a time, I decode his communications on the transference level. He arrives for the next session in gloomy, downcast mood: he has quarrelled incessantly with his wife, he doesn't want to know anything more about her, she is an impossible woman, who always wants to have the last word. At home, she told off her daughter, who shut herself in her room sobbing; he would have liked to come to the daughter's aid, but only 'she' can help her, and he even thought of beating his wife . . .

However, I do not for a moment think it appropriate to interpret all this as a response to the overdose I had administered in the previous session, so I introduce a buffer solution into the field, to dilute its acidity with unsaturated, narrative comments that grasp the trouble he must have with a 'wife' who is sometimes so unbearable. The climate improves, and he tells me that he made it up with his wife that evening, and that she had then even cooked him his favourite dish.

4

Sexuality as a narrative genre or dialect in the analyst's consulting room: a radical vertex

Psychoanalysis has made an enormous contribution to our knowledge of human sexuality since Freud's earliest works, and he himself must take the credit for having introduced the concept of psychosexuality (Freud 1905; Green 1995). The notion of 'sexual states of mind' (Meltzer 1973) has been equally fundamental. The input of psychoanalysis to theories of infantile sexual development, with the associated fantasies, sexology and the psychogenesis of sexual pathologies has become a shared heritage (Zac de Goldstein 1984; Britton 1989; Eva 1995; McDougall 1995; Sapienza 1995; Rocha Barros 1997; Eizirik 1998; Faria 1998).

This chapter, which is a further development of ideas outlined in earlier contributions of mine (Ferro 1996a, 1998d), is not about sexuality as such, but about the use of communications concerning sexuality as a means of in-depth investigation of the functioning of the human mind. I therefore focus my attention on the 'analyst's consulting room', given that almost always we have to do here with *stories* involving sexuality – that is, with narrations of, or about, sexuality.[1]

Let us consider the problem of 'what the patient and the analyst talk about'. They could be seen as talking about dislocations in time (the 'before' of Freud's theories on infantile trauma and infantile sexuality) or in space (the 'elsewhere' of theories that invoke dynamics with objects). Such theories differ radically from those in which the unconscious is regarded as something in a state of ongoing formation through processes of continuous alphabetization in the present – that is, the transformation of β-elements into α-elements. Alternatively, from my preferred vertex (which I regard as more likely to bring about transformation), 'analyst and patient' are *also* constantly talking about the present modes of functioning of the minds in the field which they constitute, which is constantly replenished by the various emotional turbulences, transferences and fantasies of the here and now (Bion 1962).

My strong assumption in this book is that patients come into analysis because they have something 'undigested' (ibid.) that must be transformed into α-elements. At any rate, this is so in favourable situations, but there may in addition be an insufficiency of the 'apparatus for thinking thoughts' (Ps ↔ D; ♀♂) (ibid.) or, in even more serious cases, a deficient α-function (Bion 1962, 1963, 1965, 1992).

The way in which this 'work' is done is continuously renarrated. In the first case (undigested facts), this operation comprises the transformation of these β-elements – or 'betalomas' (Barale and Ferro 1992) – into α-elements, which are effectively emotional pictograms; in the second case (insufficiency of the apparatus for thinking thoughts), it is the development of ♀♂ and Ps ↔ D; and in the third and most serious case (defective α-function), it entails the progressive introjection of a sounder α-function.

The patient of course chooses a narrative genre of his own, which may be a 'chronicle', a 'diaristic genre', or, in perhaps the most fortunate cases, an 'intimate diary', and so on. From the very first meeting with the analyst, and indeed even before it (Baranger and Baranger 1961–2), the patient's history and fantasies undergo narrative deconstruction. This results from the projective identifications that begin to circulate in the field, from the emotional turbulences activated within it, from the analyst's availability and 'mental space', and from his capacity for reverie and for transforming β into α.

This last process immediately becomes the engine of the analytic encounter (regardless of the analyst's chosen dialect – e.g. historical reconstruction, the internal world and internal objects, the relationship in the present, or the field) (Ferro 1996d).

The quality of functioning of the β → α process, as stated, is constantly signalled and renarrated by the patient 'in real time'. It is not difficult to understand why this should be so, both in practice and theoretically, as I shall explain below.

An α-element arising – which may also be produced by the patient's α-function – is not directly knowable except in the case of 'visual flashes' (Meltzer 1982a, 1982b, 1982c, 1984, 1986; Ferro 1992, 1993e, 1996a; Bezoari and Ferro 1992a, 1994b). Conversely, its *narrative derivatives* (Ferro 1996b, 1996d, 1996e) *are* knowable – like a picture covered by a cloth, the outline of which might be suggested through a narration (Parthenope Bion Talamo, personal communication, 1997).

Characters in the analyst's consulting room

The patient possesses a virtually infinite range of possible stories, given that he can draw on memories, fantasies, dreams, events in the real external world, what happens to himself and others, and so on. In the consulting room, we postulate that the patient's narration is not a matter of chance, but in some way unfolds with a view to communicating 'something'. This 'something' has been conceptualized in a number of different ways (Ferro 1991a, 1993b, 1993c, 1996a): (a) the facts of infancy and the family romance, (b) the facts of the internal world, and (c) relationally significant facts.

In my view, in a psychoanalytic session each of the two minds present signals to the other *in addition* the quality of their mutual interaction and functioning, as well as the degree of success of the project to transform 'undigested facts' into 'α-elements' and approximations into 'O'.

These communications are mediated by the use of characters, such as 'my father', 'my uncle' or 'my cat', which, according to the chosen vertex, are understood predominantly as (a) historical-referential characters that refer to a 'before and a now'; (b) internal-object characters that refer to an 'inside' of the patient, which may sometimes be projected 'on to' or 'into' the analyst; or (c) affective-hologram characters, which refer to modes of functioning assumed by the field in each of its sectors – characters constituting the three-dimensional fruit of the encounter between the 'waking dream thoughts' of each member of the analytic couple, in the infinite possible combinations of the characters that inhabit the couple.

From this point of view, 'my cat', for example, might signal a relational vector or sector of the field in which 'felinity' rules.

From this last vertex, each analytic session can be seen as an ongoing renarration of the emotional facts of the field (Corrao 1986). *This may occur in various dialects* – e.g. the patient's 'job', 'a love relationship' or 'a travel chronicle'.

So the boy who responded to a saturated transference interpretation by saying: 'I saw some scientists on television slicing up an egg to see how it was made inside; what a pity that stopped the chick from hatching' is thereby narrating how his α-function (or 'apparatus for thinking thoughts') 'visualized' our previous interpretation; in other words, his communication is the *narrative derivative* of a sequence of α-elements which are in themselves unknowable (but which have to do with pictograms of violence and an attack on life).

One could discuss whether we should interpret this communication directly, or 'alternatively' find a way of transforming our interpretative style so as to make it less persecutory and allow the 'chick' to hatch, while bearing in mind Bion's comment in the *Clinical Seminars* (1987: 20) that 'you can't launch out into a great explanation of the biology of the alimentary canal to a baby'.

What matters is the 'transformation' we succeed in bringing about in the field: the narrations of the field can be thought of as a Rorschach test of the couple, in which we need to pick up the 'W',[2] – that is, the emotion present at that moment, in accordance with what Bion (1963: 11) sees as the essential quality of a psychoanalytic interpretation: 'Extension in the domain of sense [,. . .] myth [, and] passion'.

For example, we could draw attention to the 'stupidity of the scientists', the uselessness of their work, or the atrocities perpetrated on the chick. In this case we should be taking up a position on Row C of the Grid, rather than giving a sterile, decoding type of interpretation in our compulsive dialect, such as: 'You're telling me that what I said to you . . .' (at the same time formulating a saturated interpretative hypothesis within ourselves, if we really need one). Instead, we should be using the patient's own dialect to proceed towards 'O' and unison with him.

Similar comments could be made about any communication of 'sexuality' in an analytic session. In other words, 'sexuality' is a character, or linkage between characters, that can be thought of as something connected with (a) a 'before' (infantile sexuality) and an 'elsewhere' (real external sexuality), as with Freud's Wolf Man; (b) an 'inside' (real internal sexuality, or sexuality of internal objects), as in Klein and her school; or (c) a narration in and of the field *in* one *of* the many 'possible dialects' of the narrative derivatives of the α-element – that is, a literary genre, which is no more, but also no less, meaningful than any other genre.

In these terms, as I have stated elsewhere (Ferro 1996a), for 'me as the analyst' sexuality in a session is the mating of minds – the 'quality' and 'modality' of the meeting of the β-element with the α-function, the handling of thoughts and their communication through the Ps $\leftrightarrow$ D oscillation, the ♀♂ interaction, and *the way in which all this is renarrated.*

What constitutes sexuality is the mode of development of ♀, which takes place through the addition of emotions that constitute the threads of the fabric of an expanding network, and of the growth of ♂, whose model is 'a medium in which lie suspended the "contents"' which protrude from an unknown base in an atmosphere of toleration of doubt (Bion 1962: 92).

Let us now consider the clinical implications of these ideas.

Martina's phimosis

Martina, a young woman who has been in analysis for some months, has often claimed to have always flown the flag of independence. One Monday, she begins her analytic week by talking about her son's 'phimosis', the concern to which it gives rise, and the operation he might need, which cannot be put off any longer.

At this point I feel permitted to tell her that there might be something in the consulting room too that remains hidden, imprisoned, and impossible to express, and that I am wondering what it may be. Taking up my comment on the fly, Martina replies instantly: 'There are some sexual things I haven't felt brave enough to bring out' – but now, however, she feels she cannot avoid doing so. She tells me that, for the last few days, she has been very pleasurably turned on when making love with her husband if he ties her up and blindfolds her. She then tells the story of Pedro Almodóvar's film whose Italian title is *Légami*, a word in which she is not sure if the first or the second syllable should be stressed.[3] It is about a man who physically ties a woman to a bed: eventually she falls deeply in love with him, and the story of the pair thereafter is of their living a life of untrammelled happiness together.

I reply that what she is telling me seems very much to call into question her idea of 'flying the flag of independence', and that she is apparently saying that she would like a relationship in which she ultimately entrusts herself to the other person, basically with consent, gives up all control of the situation, and as it were puts herself at the mercy of the 'bonds'; she hopes that a story begun 'by force' might turn into a story – the story of the analysis – that is important and alive for her.

She answers that, at this time, she feels her husband to be very close to her and very interested in her; she feels he understands her, but also recalls her profound unease during their engagement when he more or less forced her to strip, even though afterwards it had been very nice.

I am not concerned here with the subtle erotization present throughout this sequence (that is another aspect of Martina's material: she uses either erotic or intellectualistic excitation to avoid depressive experiences). My point is that the content relates – clearly, in my view – to the crisis of her (pseudo-)independence and the explicit beginnings of a relational capacity.

The yokel and the mother

A woman patient tells me that on stopping her car when she thought she might have a puncture, she felt an earth tremor; she describes some visions, including ghost-like shadows, and although she knew they originated from her own imagination, she really did see them. Then she remembers a television programme about séances.

I remember that she feels direct interpretations to be intrusive, but, since I feel these to be necessary, I say I am afraid her 'father-in-law will come along with one of his gifts', which disturb her (in the language of the analysis, the father-in-law appears whenever I actively present her with a meaning she accepts but finds intrusive). I remark that the puncture and the earth tremor put me in mind of the session we are going to miss next Monday – the session with a hole in it and the shaking up of our usual situation. I add that the ghosts suggest to me the previous day's session, in which she recalled infantile situations with her mother, 'which you experienced yesterday very intensely in your fantasy, but as if they were real'.

She replies after a moment that she has suddenly thought of Guido, a country yokel, who, when she was small, repeatedly tried to force his attentions on her too directly, to kiss her and to touch her, and how her mother had never come to her defence. I imagine that 'Guido' becomes incarnate in the field after my direct interpretations, by which she feels 'touched', and ill defended by an analyst-mother who does not prevent me, the intrusive Guido, from touching her.

Instead of making this explicit by a transference interpretation, I merely say that it must have been very painful to have a mother who did not protect her at difficult times, and I reflect that I must be more abstinent in my interpretations. After *a silence on my part* (resulting from my previous reflections), the patient says: 'You don't feel very much like working today.' Might she be afraid, I comment, that if I keep 'Guido' at bay because he is too much on top of her, touching her with over-explicit interpretations, I don't feel like working?

Patient Because I'm not used to having a mother who protects me; I don't know what it's like.

Analyst And perhaps you're afraid that more respect is a sign of distance and indifference.

Patient But it's true I'm beginning to conceive of a mother who can also act as counsel for the defence, and care for me instead of accusing me.

Who is this boy?

That is the immediate question a young colleague tells me she asked herself on her very first meeting with Berto, a small boy who was brought along for a consultation because he wanted to be a 'girl' (M. Marascutto, personal communication, 1996).

The mother tells me that she has recently separated from her husband, with whom, at the time of Berto's conception, she had been in the midst of a serious crisis: she had fallen in love with another man, and become pregnant against her will, feeling that she had been bullied into it. She had tried to abort with the morning-after pill, but it had not worked. Then she had thought: 'I'll stick up for the child and not for my husband.'

She describes Bert as unlikeable and as never having formed an attachment to her; she had once given him a finger and he had then calmed down. Already at the age of 3, he had clearly proclaimed: 'I want to be a girl.'

In a later interview, the father says the boy wants a pink room: if he wants to be gay, well, that's all right by him. He tells me that, when they went to buy a costume for Carnival, Berto at first wanted a girl's dress, but then, with some encouragement from the saleslady, opted for a Power Ranger kit.

I respond by commenting that the boy seems to have fully espoused his mother's programme. The mother, filled with rage and hate for her husband, had no space for all of the boy, so that her husband's emotional genetic heritage, the 'Y', as it were remained outside . . . To find a place in his mother's mind, Berto had to act like a contortionist, but the 'Y' – what came from the father – remained outside, at least seemingly, in terms of masculine identity as well as in other respects.

There is no room for him. Even if he is helped, the Power Ranger comes out – with all the rage and hate of the embryonic virile identity that basically succeeded in resisting the abortion. This description is of course to be understood in mental terms.

Figure 7 Berto's drawing of a lawn, little flowers, a chest and a bed

My colleague now shows me the first drawings made by Berto in his sessions. One sheet of paper contains several very girlish sketches, depicting a lawn, some little flowers, a chest, a bed (Figure 7) and a paper figure of a girl with a huge three-dimensional paper dummy in her mouth (Figure 8).

On lifting the lid of the chest (Figure 9), one immediately sees the outline of a boy, with testicles, a penis and trousers; raising the blanket on the bed reveals a sheet and pillow that had concealed an enormous penis; and the three-dimensional dummy is nothing other than an enormous penis.

So there we have it: all the emotions, projective identifications, rage and hate that have found no place in his mother's mind have remained there without being alphabetized, and he must 'suck them himself'. The girl is nothing other than the mask (and Berto also makes a mask) of a Power Ranger, or perhaps also of a furious Genghis Khan, looking for the place he is entitled to – as we may infer from a subsequent drawing of a pirate's hat peeking out of a masked face (Figure 10).

Lauretta

Lauretta is often embarrassed at the sexual material that occurs to her during her sessions. She now has a problem: her husband would like to make love from behind, and *he* says that she wants this too. But the idea terrifies her: she is afraid of ending up torn apart and bleeding at Accident & Emergency.

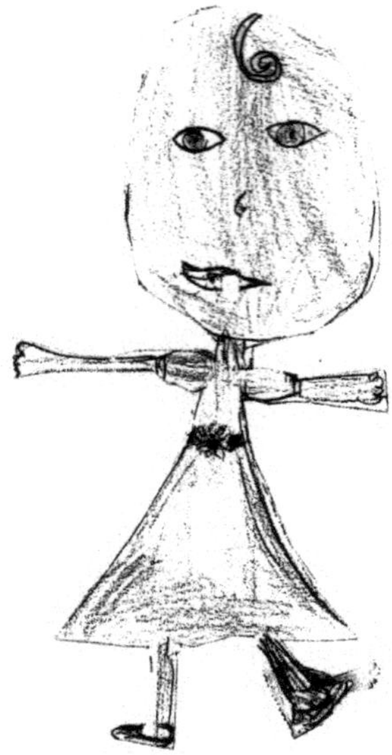

Figure 8 Drawing of a girl with a huge three-dimensional paper dummy (not visible in the figure)

Figure 9 Inside the chest, and underneath the blanket on the bed

Figure 10 Berto's drawing of a masked face

It occurs to me that last week she felt bad after an interpretation of mine on a subject which the patient felt to be taboo and had for a long time avoided. So I tell her that I wonder if her problem is whether to let herself go in the analysis, in the relationship 'from behind' with me, and whether to do so with trust or in terror in case I tear her apart with what I say.

She now describes the plot of a splendid film she has seen, *Mary Reilly*,[4] which recounts the story of Dr Jekyll and Mr Hyde through the eyes of a young housemaid. This enables me to tell her that, shoulder on, it is hard to know who is behind one: 'Dr Ferro or Mr Iron.'[5] Laughing, she answers: 'But I think my husband loves and understands me.'

Theoretical considerations: α-elements and their narrative derivatives

Let me now return to, and expand on, the points I made at the beginning of the previous chapter, where I noted that Bion postulates the existence of a constant mental activity (the α-function) that syncretizes all forms of afferences from the sense organs in a visual element (the α-element). These visual elements are stated to be formed continuously and sequentially.

To give as simple as possible an example, in a game of *Memory*,[6] one sequence of cards might be flower-cherry-mosquito. These might be pictograms of an experience that is at first pleasant, then tasty, and subsequently becomes vaguely irritating – as in, say, a relational short film about a couple of people who are speaking, remaining silent, or doing something . . . or an analytic couple.

According to the various sensory perceptions that continue to flood in, further movie frames constantly form. As these elements gradually come into being, they may, as in an imaginary game of *Memory*, be turned either up, in which case they form the system of consciousness, or down, forming the unconscious system.

In other words, the unconscious is located not upstream but downstream of the encounter between the β-element (proprioception-exteroception) and the α-function; that is to say – again using the *Memory* metaphor – it too is made up of face-down α-elements. However, the unconscious may also be inhabited by what Bion calls 'undigested facts', which are accumulations of emotional or sensory-perceptual proto-tensions that have not been transformed into visual elements and thereby digested and made thinkable. These undigested facts are not β-elements, but can be seen as partly digested and metabolized βs ('balpha-elements').[7]

The α-element, or sequence of α-elements flower-cherry-mosquito, is not directly knowable except in two cases:

(a) When the α-element, a frame from the 'waking dream thought' film, escapes from the apparatus that was supposed to contain it and is projected and seen on the outside. In this case a patient might, say, see a flower, a cherry or a mosquito, which syncretizes his mental state at that relational instant.
(b) When we can come into contact with, and directly 'visualize', the α-element – that is, when using our capacity for 'reverie', in which an image, which is usually well protected, comes up and can be seen with the 'mind's eye'; this is the maximum level of contact a mind can achieve with itself.

A characteristic of the α-element is that it is pictographed in real time, and syncretized absolutely unpredictably; that is to say, it is not formed using predetermined symbols, but is on each occasion a unique and unrepeatable work of poetry and pictorial art.

An example of the first situation is the alarmed response of one of my female patients to the announcement of an increase in my fees: 'I see a chicken being plucked.' The α-element, or visual movie frame, had slipped out and become visible. If we watch out for these phenomena, described previously by Meltzer (1982a, 1982b, 1984), we find that they are much more frequent than we might have imagined.

The second situation can be exemplified by a session that seemed to me incomprehensibly banal, in which I 'saw' a cemetery with graves. This enabled me to get in touch with a patient's deeply buried depressive anxieties, and to find the correct register to enable me to make contact with his suicidal intentions, by linking the content of my reverie with what he was telling me.

The style, quality and pictorial genre of the α-element are specific to each human individual; they constitute the mind's most fundamental nucleus of truth in relation to one's emotions and perceptions. An α-element is always 'private', and not in any way generalizable.

Normally, however, patients do not project their α-elements, and analysts are not always capable of reverie. So are α-elements inaccessible except through these two narrow channels?

By no means: mental life, the root of thought, is made up of α-elements, of which we can know the *narrative derivatives* that constantly bud forth in the stories told in the consulting room by virtue of the *narrative capacity of minds in the waking state* (the apparatus for thinking thoughts).

'Flower-cherry-mosquito' might lead to the patient's bringing material whose 'concentrate' or 'essence' (flower-cherry-mosquito) is dissolved in a narration. If the here and now of the field is a pleasant experience that becomes tasty and then vaguely irritating, *that* may be narrated in an *infinity* of possible genres:

(a) *A memory of infancy*: 'When I was small, I always looked forward to my grandparents coming with sweets, but then I got angry because I always had to wait till dinner time to eat them.'
(b) *A seemingly external diaristic genre*: 'Today my wife opened the door to me with gusto and you could see she was happy, but then I got alarmed when she told me about my sister-in-law's phone call.'
(c) *A sexual genre*: 'Making love to Giulia used to be very satisfying; what a pity her aloofness irritated me.'

We could go on with (d), (e), (f), (g), (h), . . . (y), (z), all of which are different narrative embodiments of the same emotional experience: flower-cherry-mosquito.

From this point of view, 'sexuality' is a choice of narrative genre and is to the α-element as the plot is to the fabula.[8] Furthermore, an α-element too can pictograph an emotional experience sexually. So there are two loci of sexual images: the α-element itself, and its associated narrative genre.

What is the origin of the sequence of α-elements? The answer is obvious: it is the *here and now of the emotional field*, of which it becomes an indicator. The transferences and fantasies constituting the matrix and engine of the analysis flow together in it; hence it is the *here and now* of the emotional field that is transformed into α and then narrated.

However, not everything proceeds so smoothly. The creative activity of the analytic couple and of every mind is constantly put to the test by the arrival of quantities of β- or balpha-elements (the latter, as stated earlier, being regurgitated, partially digested elements). As a result, a sequence becomes: flower-cherry-mosquito/β or balpha turbulence. Turbulences of β- or balpha-elements raise the issue of the capacity of the minds in question to form other α-elements consistent with these turbulences and capable of conferring meaning on them. 'Scimitar-lion-lake', for example, might signify a relational mode that suggests something cutting, which becomes dangerous and then calms down.

The situation is not always so favourable: instead of the transformation β (or balpha) $\rightarrow \alpha$, the turbulence may persist, or even increase, giving rise to evacuations.

The above remarks have to do with the field and its movements during waking life.[9] However, there is of course another channel of access to the α-element – namely, the 'royal road' of night dreams and their narration. These were addressed in Bezoari and Ferro (1992a) and are also discussed in the next chapter.

Concluding remarks

Communications in analysis have to do with the 'analytic field', and tell of this and nothing else, even if the mode of analyst–patient interaction can be narrated in an infinite number of dialects. Why, I wonder, should this 'analytic vertex' not apply if a male patient mentions the 'dryness of his wife's vagina', or a female patient her husband's 'premature ejaculation' that prevents her from having passionate feelings when they make love, or a teenager a flasher 'displaying his wares' outside her school?

The assumption that these or similar communications are of interest to us in relation only to 'actual sexuality' and not to the 'sexuality of the consulting room' is in my view likely to kill off the specificity of the 'analytical laboratory'. By the 'sexuality of the consulting room' I mean, for example in the case of the 'dry vagina', a possible dryness assumed by a particular area of the field, making the relationship painful in the absence of appropriate lubrication; the premature ejaculation might suggest an over-hasty explicit interpretation of meanings that takes away the taste for sharing – that is, the presence in the field of an 'incontinent part' that needs to be transformed so that it becomes capable of containing and hence of feeling and experiencing passion; and the flasher points to the revelation of excessively raw contents that can only cause disorientation. All these examples should be seen as mere 'exercises', because in a field-based approach it is of course impossible to decode a communication, but only to generate meanings that progressively develop and become interlinked (Borgogno 1997; Gaburri 1997; Vallino Macciò 1997).

In these terms, in the consulting room 'we are constantly having sex and nothing but sex'– in the sense, of course, that we relate to each other, and that this relationship *is sex*, even if it follows from the necessary rules of abstinence that we have 'chaste' sex. However, it is certainly not chaste with regard to the emotions activated and experienced, and to the fantasizing, also in sexual terms, of the continuous matings *between minds* – the sexuality of the vicissitudes of ♀♂ and $\beta \rightarrow \alpha$.

Analysis, of course, is not an end in itself, but is intended to bring about far-reaching transformations in those who have recourse to it. In the case of the lady whose 'husband' suffers from premature ejaculation, it could, for example, serve to 'transform' the incontinent part of herself that forces her to marry a premature ejaculator so as to find a way of experiencing her own problem of incontinence (and in the appropriate circumstances narrating it); or, having once acquired the capacity for containment, she may no longer be able to carry on with her husband in such a way as to favour the occurrence of his symptom. There is an infinite range of other possibilities, but the 'husband's' premature ejaculation is treated in the analyst's consulting room, just as the symptom of 'being unable to keep one's files in order at the office' would be treated there.

Once the problem is solved in the consulting room following transformational operations there, these will necessarily reverberate outside, but this outside, for us as analysts, is somewhere 'outside the field', to which we may have access like anyone else, but no longer as 'analysts' – because, for us as analysts, anywhere 'outside the field' is inevitably also 'out of play'.

To possess the status of an analyst, the analyst must be alive, and must have both a patient who is alive and a functioning setting; outside this context, the analyst is a man or woman who is entitled to express a view on anything, but not specifically as an analyst.

This is not to deny our common, shared history, to which I referred earlier, and our gratitude for the theories and models that constitute our 'highest common factors', on which we must never tire of reflecting. However, this entails using what we know – as suggested by the title of Roberto Speziale-Bagliacca's fine book *On the Shoulders of Freud* (1982), but I could also add the names of Klein, Bion or any of our other masters – in order to see something that is highly specific today with regard to the field that is constantly enlarged in the process of psychoanalytic exploration (Bion), a field in which other vertices, other organizational possibilities, other models, and other theories always coexist.

To sum up, there are different clinical as well as theoretical models, and the fundamental aspect of one of these is *memory*, with all its complex interlinkages and vicissitudes. Remembering is an antidote to repeating. Repeating enables us to open the door to memory: memory is the guarantor of the remembered reality, although there may also be deeper-lying memories, alternating dialectically with screen memories.

Another model focuses on the internal objects and their vicissitudes. It is vitally important to pick up the patient's anxiety and to uncover the fantasies underlying the mutual relations between the internal objects, many of which may gradually come to be projected on to the analyst.

The central aspect of yet another model is the interrelationship between the patient's and the analyst's 'waking dream thought'. What is important here is the constant construction and deconstruction of these dream thoughts, a process that yields the *figures of the field* whereby the 'field' is constantly narrated.

Readers will be familiar with my interest in the characters of the session. It follows from the very structure of the models mentioned above that, in the first, the characters will be understood predominantly as such and hence as belonging to the patient's real external and past history, and that they will, if anthropomorphic, refer to 'persons'. In the second model, the characters will be manifestations of the 'internal objects' and therefore indicative of fantasies. In the third model, the characters will be a token of the need for 'narrative nodes', whereby the linking of the narration of the mutual functioning and interaction of the patient's and analyst's minds becomes possible; they will be what I have called functional aggregates or affective holograms.

Of course, these three models arise according to the analyst's chosen position; in a field context, they may coexist and be linked to each other in an infinite variety of ways.

While all this is obviously true of anthropomorphic characters, it applies equally to any 'non-anthropomorphic character', however insignificant, as well as to the relations between characters.

The 'penis', 'making love to', 'premature ejaculation', and indeed also 'my husband', 'my son' or 'my cat', will lead different existences in each of the three models. In the first, the penis, or making love, will refer to the 'real penis' or to acted-out sexuality; in the second they will relate to the relevant early fantasies; and in the third they will be figures in the story who will renarrate places in or modes of functioning of the field.

5

The waking dream: theoretical and clinical aspects

In my view, we should be just as interested in oneiric manifestations in an analytic session as we are in night dreams brought after the event like a recorded television programme. Dream-like manifestations in the session are one of the pillars of Bion's thought: in waking life as in sleep, there is a kind of 'dreaming', which is what enables us to form α-elements, to establish the contact barrier and to distinguish conscious from unconscious (Bion 1962, 1963, 1965).

Before considering these matters in detail, let me say that this chapter constitutes a continuation and deepening of the ideas put forward in an article by Bezoari and myself that I consider to be still valid today (Bezoari and Ferro 1992a). In it, we examined in succession the main psychoanalytic conceptions of 'dreams', starting with the famous dream of the Wolf Man (Freud 1914), which, we said, we were tempted 'to see as a precise description, from the vertex assumed by the patient at that time, of the nature of his experience of what was happening in the analyst's consulting room'. We acknowledged Freud's extraordinary capacity to tell the patient a story and, albeit without realizing the full extent of the violence of the relationship in the here and now (from the patient's vertex), to bring about a narrative transformation (Corrao 1991) that conferred a credible, digested and assimilable form to the patient's terror and panic at the wolf's claws concealed behind the 'paw made white at the baker's' (Freud 1913: 286).

We then turned to the interpretative model we deduced from the work of Abraham and Klein, drawing attention to the risk of establishment of a code or, in narratological terms, of a 'rigid encyclopedia'. This led us to emphasize the revolution brought about by Bion, for whom dreams are re-elaborated samples of an ongoing process occurring throughout both sleep and waking life, and are placed in a relational space, as in a mother's reverie with regard to her child's projective identifications.

We then considered the relational aspect of dreams and their narration, on the basis of the work of Baranger and Baranger (1961–2) and Meltzer (1967,

1984). We went on to examine the problem of gradients of alphabetization, from hallucination to transformations into hallucinosis, oneiric 'film frames' and dreams (Ferro 1993e). A focal point of our interest was the oneiric 'film frame' and its auditory equivalent (and, I would now add, its coenaesthetic equivalent), as well as, implicitly, the 'narrative derivatives of the α-element'.

Our article ended with a consideration of the problem of the 'translation' or 'construction' of dreams and the possibility of regarding them as 'open works' *par excellence*.

The issue I now wish to address, based on Bion's concept of the 'α-dream', is the origin of the patient's communications. These, of course, draw on his history, as brought into the present in the transference; equally obviously, they have to do with his internal world and the associated fantasies, and are projected into the here and now of the analytic situation. I should like to add a further aspect to these clinical and theoretical certainties of ours – namely, that from a vertex different from but coexisting with the others, they may be regarded as real-time responses derived from the waking dream thought in continuous formation (Ferro 1991b, 1993b, 1993c, 1994c, 1996a, 1996d).

In search of the α-element (the protovisual element of thought)

As stated in the previous chapters, Bion (1962, 1992) postulates the continuous formation of α-elements in waking life. These visual elements, which arise continuously and sequentially, are not directly knowable except in two situations: the visual flash and reverie (as well as, of course, in night dreams). Outside these two situations, we can know the 'narrative derivatives of the α-elements' (Ferro 1996c, 1998c).

From my present preferred vertex, it is the *here and now* of the emotional field that is transformed into α and hence narrated; these narrative derivatives thus become indicators that signal, within the field, the patient's mental functioning and the progress of the ongoing relational situation, enabling us to modulate our interpretations continuously.

Before considering the narrative derivatives of the α-elements in detail, I should like briefly to recapitulate the situations in which direct contact with them is possible.

Visual flashes

As we know, these occur whenever an α-element – that is, a frame from the film of waking dream thought – escapes from the apparatus that was supposed to contain it and is projected and seen outside. They thus constitute a hot line to what is happening in the flasks of the mind's laboratory.

Reverie

As we have seen, we can sometimes come into contact with the α-element and 'visualize' it directly. In reverie, an image that is usually thoroughly protected appears on the surface and can be seen with 'the mind's eye'; this is the maximum level of contact a mind can make with itself.

Dreams

The foregoing relates to the field and its movements in waking life. However, there is of course another channel of access to α-elements – namely, the 'royal road' of night dreams and their telling in the analytic session (Freud 1900; Mancia 1994a, 1994b). Night dreams differ greatly from α-elements in that the former perform the function of sorting and filtering (redreaming – Catz de Katz 1996) what has been constantly 'filmed', alphabetized and preserved during waking life (Bianchedi 1995). At this point it is as if, at the end of each day, we possessed myriads of α-elements stored in various ways.

There are then two possibilities. First, in the absence of significant sensory afferences, there may be an *α-metafunction* which, in this situation, acts on the α-elements to form a syncretic narrative mosaic of the emotionally salient facts. Second, it may be hypothesized that, just as there is an 'apparatus for thinking thoughts' (Bion 1962) that operates on thoughts in waking life once these have been formed from α-elements (an 'apparatus' described by Bion as made up of ♀♂ and Ps ↔ D), so there is an 'apparatus for dreaming dreams', which acts as it were on a second level on all the stored α-elements to supply a figurative narration that confers meaning on experiences on the basis of criteria of urgency.

I would describe this 'apparatus for dreaming dreams', which necessarily draws on the collected α-elements, as the 'narrative capacity of the dreaming mind' – a kind of directorial function applied to the equally creative, but instant-by-instant, work of the cameraman who forms the α-elements.

It should now be clear that much of our work is done on highly creative material produced by the patient: α-elements, narrative derivatives of α-elements in waking life, and very sophisticated directorial sorting and assembly of α-elements (i.e. dreams). We also work with emotional turbulences, β-elements, lies and evacuated thoughts.

A seeming digression: an α-element?

For the sake of clarity, I have grossly oversimplified my exemplification of α-elements. In reality, an α-element not only is pictographed in real time and syncretized absolutely unpredictably, but also poetically syncretizes all ongoing emotional experience, instant by instant.

At our first meeting, a borderline adolescent described to me certain images he was seeing at that moment, and said he had tried to draw one of them for me (Figure 11). This is the only occasion when a patient has drawn me a 'visual flash', and it is the closest thing to an α-element (or an agglomerate of α-elements) I have been able to find. It seems to me to sum up pictographically everything activated in him on our first meeting: the monster . . . the terror of being devoured . . . Zorro with his mask . . . an Arab archer . . . Cupid . . . something mysterious and unknown . . . a nest . . . the devil . . . aggression . . . relief . . . hope (the little

Figure 11 Drawing of a visual flash

man at the bottom saying 'I miss you') . . . castration anxiety . . . not knowing how to go on . . . the foreshortened limbs . . . not knowing how to relate and what to expect . . . All these aspects are 'syncretized' in the single α-element, and will have to be correlated with the patient's subsequent products and those of the analyst, so as gradually to allow the sharing of what is initially still too dense and saturated, although opening the way to an infinity of meanings.

What I have sought to explain in terms of Bion's theory of α-elements and the α-function is admirably exemplified by Robert Louis Stevenson's (1892) attribution of his creative activity to 'Little People' dwelling inside him, who are the authors of his artistic creations: they work away inside him in both sleep and waking life, and thereafter regale him without his knowledge with the fruits of their precious labours.

Narrative derivatives of α-elements: film sets and screenplays in the process of continuous transformation

However, as stated earlier, we do not normally have patients who project their α-elements, or analysts who are always capable of reverie – so are α-elements unattainable except by way of these two narrow channels?

By no means: mental life, the root of thought, is made up of these α-elements, and we can acquaint ourselves with their narrative derivatives, which constantly bud forth in the tales told in the analyst's consulting room, through the *narrative capacity* of our minds while awake (the apparatus for thinking thoughts).

The sequence 'flower-cherry-mosquito' mentioned in the previous chapter would thus be embodied in material in which the 'concentrate' or 'essence' (flower-cherry-mosquito) is dissolved in the patient's narration, as illustrated in the following clinical vignettes.

The absence of Sollievo

Aware of how sensitively Marco reacts to any communication about separations, I tried to find a suitable way of telling him my holiday dates and thought I had succeeded.

Marco begins the next session by telling me how well he is getting on with his wife, and conveys the sad news that Professor Sollievo has retired. A dream then follows: alone beside a sea with mountainous waves, he is afraid there will be a flood; next he is with his brother on a muddy, uphill country road; then he is with his parents in a house high above sea level when a huge boulder comes crashing down; although at first he fears serious consequences, luckily it falls some distance away without doing any damage.

I think of a possible interpretation about the holidays and about the absence of *sollievo*.[1] While I am wondering how to present to the patient the – at least to me – obvious contents of the dream (the emotional wave and the feared collapse after my telling him my holiday dates), a few moments pass before I am able to interpret, during which the patient says: 'My wife wants to be turned on; when we make love, she wants not only foreplay but fore-foreplay.' I feel that I can delay no longer, but, not yet having a well-cooked interpretation ready, I try some interpretative approaches. In response to the patient's comment 'My wife is sometimes too seductive and likes to play', I interpret the absence of *sollievo* (relief) and the dreams as a response to the holiday communication. He answers: 'My friend Ferrazzo always puts on airs; he's almost unbearable.'

The point I am making is that the patient 'responds' to every emotional movement of the analyst with real-time pictograms, and that the 'response' is therefore *a narrative derivative of waking dream thought* – that is, of the sequence of α-elements pictographed in response to the interpretative stimulus.

The aunt's fall

Analyst (giving a reconstructive interpretation): The relationship with your father, which left you feeling abandoned and betrayed, echoes on in your other relationships.
Patient (after a moment's silence): My aunt fell down the stairs and bumped her head . . . I'm wondering what to do about school; I feel that it's my work, that I like it and that it interests me . . . The problem is the cost. (The patient misses the next session.)

In other words, the patient has pictographed α-elements connected with not being held, with feeling hurt, with pain, with wondering what to do, with the acknowledgement of interest, and . . . with the emotional cost. The unknowable α-elements have come on to the stage by way of a narration that parallels them: 'What you are telling me comes as a surprise; it is like a blow on the head that hurts . . . it interests me a lot and really is the work I would like to do, but the emotional cost is high.'

The injured puppy . . . and the knitting

I cancel Rita's Friday session. After missing her session on the following Monday, she comes along for her Tuesday session. She says she had to miss the Monday session because she was taking care of a puppy that had been run over. She took it to a vet for an operation, which turned out to be long and laborious, and in the end the vet told her he had no room for the injured puppy, so she had to stay home and look after it, as it had to be fed every three hours. She tried but failed to find someone to look after it for her.

She asks me not to be angry with her for not having come, as her boyfriend has already told her off. I say only that there are situations in which the vet and a puppy's life are more important than an analytic session. The patient is greatly reassured and continues her account of the operation performed by the vet and the subsequent care of the puppy; she emerges from the state of persecutory confusion she was in at the beginning of the session.

Towards the end, when I feel the patient is no longer persecuted, I tell her that perhaps, looking at the situation from inside the analysis, I was the one who ran over the puppy, by cancelling the session, and that her missing the Monday session had been the painful but necessary 'operation' for treating a serious injury.

She begins the next session by telling me that she has had two dreams; in the first, she makes a fine piece of embroidery, sells it and uses the proceeds to take care of some Indian children, while in the second she receives an abusive telephone call.

I of course see the dreams as her way of pictorially syncretizing the emotional quality of the previous session: the long 'embroidery' and then my interpretation. I say only that it is hard to produce a nice piece of embroidery if she then gets abusive telephone calls. I also think the patient believes that it is better to lick one's own wounds, that she cannot yet trust in the possibility of using me to help her make a better job her embroidery, and I ask: 'But do you only embroider, or can you also crochet, or knit with *ferri*?'[2] She bursts out laughing; she has understood the meaning of my intervention, and launches into a long description of the beauty and usefulness of working with *ferri* . . . she has bought lots of balls of wool . . . and begun knitting a sweater.

The 'intoxicated' analyst

Following an apparently good session with a seriously disturbed woman patient, I feel disorientated and confused. The next patient tells me of her memory of her 'father's death', of experiences of loneliness and loss, and I suddenly realize how mentally absent I am. She goes on to tell me about an acquaintance suffering from *alcohol-induced cirrhosis*, and it is only then that I become aware that I have come out of the previous session like a drunk. Even though I have got in touch with my mental state, induced by the session with the seriously disturbed woman, the *next* patient also tells me at one point about a friend she sometimes finds drunk.

Now at last I succeed in absorbing all the 'alcohol' and resuming my normal 'trim': the stage fills with other characters who indicate to me that I have recovered my normal level of mental functioning. It is obvious to me that, through narrative derivatives, patients are constantly and unconsciously signalling what they syncretize in α-elements, and continuously renarrating it through characters and screenplays that tell us how the present-day relationship and their internal worlds and history intersect in the field.

This process of continuous renarration of the emotional movements of the couple in the analytic field can of course be mediated not only by the narrative derivatives of α-elements during waking life but also through night dreams narrated after the event in the session like the playback of a recorded TV programme.

Anna's sweater and her open window

At the beginning of a session, a woman patient tells me a dream: she is in a car with a female friend, who drops her (the patient's) sweater out of the window, so they have to turn back laboriously and search for it among brambles, thorns and woods. She spontaneously associates to a childhood memory of her sister holding a designer headscarf of hers (the patient's) out of the car window and letting go of it; after a scene when they got home, the sister said the scarf had got lost; the father then turned back to look for it and eventually found it.

I ask the patient what it is, of all the things we discussed in the previous session, that has flown away and got lost. Crying, she calls herself a 'moaner' and childish. I can see how laborious it is to 'turn back'. I tell her it seems to me important to turn back and recover what we have lost. After a long silence, she tells me through her tears that she felt I was not paying equal attention to everything she was telling me, and that I was letting some things slip away as if they were of no consequence, such as what she said about . . . she then enumerates the things I had neglected to take up.

Robin Hood's arrows

A woman patient dreams of a fight between Hercules and Robin Hood. Hercules thrusts a javelin into Robin Hood's back, but Robin does not lose heart and goes on shooting arrows at Hercules, wounding him.

This dream can surely be nothing other than a narration in images of the previous session, in which I hurt the patient with an unexpected transference interpretation; she then took her revenge by shooting lots of little arrows at me and trying to inflict some wounds. My interpretation to this effect gives rise to a number of expansions, extending out from the here and now in unforeseeable directions. Hence interpretation of the here and now must be seen not as a destination but as a point of departure for unknown expansions.

The unreliable nanny and the absent-minded surgeon

A patient tells me she had a terrible fit of anxiety while buying ricotta at the grocer's. She then brings two dreams. In the first, her little girl, who had been entrusted to an unreliable nanny, falls down the stairs, bumps her head after plunging down a few steps, and fractures her foot. The patient rushes down to take her daughter, now in a coma, into her arms, and searches desperately for her own parents, who, when she finds them, listen to her but seem not to see her. She then goes to a hospital, where some surgeons have left a threaded needle, as one might do when making a sweater, on the edge of an enormous wound in the little girl's belly. In the second dream, she senses the presence of a thief in her house; on meeting him she is terrified, as he is a potential murderer who might kill her.

Licia is a patient who suffers from 'panic attacks', and the above sequence in my view tells us a great deal: the manifest scene (buying the ricotta – going to analysis) is permeated with emotions stemming from other levels on which the vicissitudes of the analysis are narrated.

The end of the session is like a violent plunge down the stairs, after which she discovers herself with her own infantile part in a coma, with no one to help her. The analyst ends the session indifferently, as one might leave off one's knitting with a view to resuming work on it later, disregarding the pain thereby inflicted. He is at the same time the thief feared by the patient, especially now the Easter holidays are approaching, when he will rob her of her sessions – but he is also a potential murderer, killing her with his deeply disturbing interpretations.

This last aspect emerges from the patient's associations to her terror of doctors and their indifference to other people's pain, and to her fear that I might deprive her of sessions – as well as the other constant fear that, if she exposes herself by telling me her most intimate feelings, I might 'kill' her with my response.

If this deeper level of a seemingly good and simple relationship is not constantly negotiated, emotions that are apparently meaningless and 'out of context' burst on to the scene. However, if this deeper level is plumbed, the profound emotions, panic and terror are given a meaning and context, and may attain thinkability.

A homosexual relationship

A female patient has great difficulty in talking about things she feels are very intimate. In a difficult and stormy session, after keeping these inside her for a long time, she manages with great difficulty to express them in a climate of increasing closeness.

Next day she brings two dreams. In the first, she has a homosexual relationship with a woman friend, and in the second she is looking for a male friend, but then along comes his present girlfriend and stops her from getting near him. Eventually, though, she succeeds in getting rid of her and finding the male friend, with whom she has a very satisfying talk.

There are various ways of seeing these dreams. One might theorize a development from a symbiotic-perverse situation to a more adult, oedipal one – from a relationship with a fusional mother to an oedipal conflictuality in which the mother is also her rival.

However, there is also a more creative possibility: the dreams can instead be seen as being about the emotions aroused by the previous day's session; from an autoerotic, masturbatory situation in which the patient was able to tell her personal things only to herself, she has been able to move on to one in which, despite the difficulty, she has become able to communicate and narrate intimate matters to another person.

A pair of hands stolen from the land

Rosanna, a psychologist from a university team, says she has had a dream. By way of introduction, she tells me she has dreamed of an impulsive patient, Tamone, who, being dim-witted but having a good pair of hands, gets himself accepted at 'Ruralia', a rehabilitation centre where people work on the land. In the dream, she goes to Ruralia to talk to the staff in charge of Tamone, but is astonished to find Tamone himself there, dressed as a member of the staff with a jacket and tie, quite unlike his usual appearance. At this point she notices needles of varying lengths stuck into her hand; they hurt and make her feel as if she has been crucified. But Tamone has really changed, you can be sure of that.

This dream follows a session in which the patient complained that I have given a transference interpretation of some criticisms she expressed about her sister-in-law, and I replied that perhaps she was right to be irritated if I did not take sufficient account of what she told me but instead immediately interpreted it as something intimately connected with me.

I am now able to interpret the dream without difficulty. The analyst (the dim-witted Tamone) becomes someone who needs to be cared for and who does indeed need to work at *Ruralia*, but then Rosanna is impressed by my acknowledgement of the legitimacy of her protest, although she wonders whether she can be sure of it, whether it really is a change in me that she can rely on . . . or whether I shall go on wounding her with the needles of my interpretations, by which she sometimes feels crucified. I add that the protagonist's name is significant, containing as it does the sequence *amo* [I love], which is still there even at difficult moments.

Impressed by this interpretation of the dream, Rosanna is now able to tell me more about the 'sister-in-law' – that she fails to respond to real needs (I had just told her that I could not accede to her request to change the time of a session) and is deaf to emotional demands . . . unlike Aunt Linda, who, by contrast . . . In other words, we are witnessing a return to the stage of these 'characters' who stand for 'relational vectors' in the field, but this cannot yet be explicitly interpreted in the field in relational terms, as that would be like 'sticking needles in her' instead of instilling trust and well-being.

What is not in the relationship is nevertheless there in the present field of the emotions, and of their narrations and transformations in the analyst's consulting room. The aspect of containment/non-containment obviously has to do with Rosanna's psychic life, but emotions can be transformed only in the field, before being reintrojected into the internal world so that they can inhabit the patient's history.

Fabrizio's Chinese boxes

Fabrizio is a patient who brings his entire family to life in the consulting room. The characters he brings over and over again immediately suggest modes of functioning (both his own and mine) that come alive in the room, often mutually unintegrated.

With this patient, I find myself in the room with a jealous man, with a woman who is 'offended' by the slightest interpretation, with a teenage girl who does not speak (he won't speak to me, misses sessions and acts out), and with a delicate boy who continues to suffer from every trauma. My problem has been how to interpret in this context.

I work with characters as I would in a child analysis, using cows, sheep or lions . . . I try to keep my interventions unsaturated and open, so as to allow the patient to contribute actively . . . I take care 'not to wound him' in any way, and avoid upsetting or wounding him with the traumas of my interpretations.

A patient who brings other people's dreams, adapting them to her own expressive needs

In the last session before the holidays, Rossella, a patient at an advanced stage of her analysis, brings some of her children's dreams: as Fernando is about to cross a road, a Tutsi with a spear gets out of a car and tries to run him through with it, but then Uncle Bernardo comes along and breaks the Tutsi's spear; Fernando can then cross the road with his uncle . . . Luigi dreams that he is being pursued by a lion; he has to keep on running and running, and finally escapes when Uncle Bernardo comes along and saves him . . .

The persecution anxiety induced by the forthcoming holiday break encounters an analytic function that has already been partially introjected and, in the manner of Saint Bernard (Bernardo), protects her when crossing difficult and dangerous terrain.

Semi (1998) likewise describes a patient's use of a friend's dream, reported in her session.

Free associations

Free associations can be thought of as potential carriers enabling one to approach and draw on elements of the *dream work of the moment*; this means that they are actually obligatory associations derived from the (oneiric!) resultant of the emotional climate of the moment. Hence Bion's view that we can be conscious only of feelings in the *present*. That is why free associations reveal the meaning of dreams, but they do so in the sense of making a further contribution in the here and now to the sampling of the emotional-oneiric climate of the moment (that is to say, they are the narrative derivatives of the α-elements produced in the dream).

The foregoing implies a blurring of the distinction between dreams and other forms of communication, so that an entire gradient of oneiricity is present in every communication (in a continuum from dreams to hallucinations). Whereas an α-function is indeed at work, so too is dream thought during waking life (except in situations when the mind is 'dismantled') – or, as Bion would say, α-dreaming is active.

Does the container hold fast or does it tear open?

The interpretation of patients' waking material is often felt to be 'not all the patient's own work' and as such gives rise to immune defences, whereas dreams represent a more accessible pathway, precisely because they *are* all the patient's own work.

What if the 'keloid' fails?

In a session with Giovanni, now in his tenth year of analysis, I have occasion to tell him that many of his ways of relating, which are like those of a Mafia clan, put me in mind of keloids, or extensive areas of scar tissue, which suggest the existence of a wound and of a consequent deep sensitivity. Next time he brings a dream: he is in a jungle with wild animals like lions or tigers; all of a sudden his gun is taken away from him, leaving him defenceless and at the mercy of the animals' ferocity. Then, in another sequence, beside the label on his letter-box, he finds another name – the name of an unknown person, which actually frightens him. In yet another dream, he is first with a boy he is fond of, called Piero, then with the film director Buñuel whose plots are so perverse, and finally in a harem with the Shah of Persia.

All these stories foreshadow a possible 'catastrophic change' when the 'keloid' is plunged into crisis.

It is always a matter of proportion

Following many years of analysis with Elisa, it finally becomes possible for us to talk to each other directly and explicitly. After one of these sessions, she dreams of being attacked by a man who violently attacks her, as in a news item she has seen in which an Israeli breaks a Palestinian's arm with a rock.

Words can hurt, but now she can see me explicitly not only as an Israeli, but also as a yokel and a dwarf; we are able to talk about everything that has had to remain unsaid between us, such as the old fear that compelled her, when going out with others, to take Reasec, a well-known antidiarrhoeal agent, in case she became incontinent of faeces – or rather, in case she were to let slip some stupid remark – just as she had been 'contained' in her sexual and relational life too.

Interpretation and narration

Gustavo brings a dream of a girl he finds very attractive indeed, but two people prevent him from getting close to her . . . then he compiles an expert's report on a palmar aponeurosis, and finally there are lots of characteropaths, sociopaths, people who have committed every crime in the book, especially murder, in a court room where the disfigured, hirsute judge looks like a criminal himself.

He also says it is in relating to other people that he becomes aware of difficulties, as violent emotional storms soon arise in him.

I could interpret this in terms of our relationship, telling him that he would like to have an intense love relationship with me, but that something stops him: I could tell him that he not only engages in a kind of masturbatory activity, but also relates to me as a criminal might relate to an utterly harsh judge, and that the terror of a mutual relationship made up of accusation, bullying and violence, in which I criminalize his 'staying in bed' and keep phoning to cancel sessions, seems to prevail over the affectionate climate of a good relationship that he would like. However, I feel it will be more profitable to let *him* develop lines of association that will lead us to new scripts, which could never be written if I were to give a saturated interpretation of this kind (Guignard 1998).

A place for dreams

I have mentioned elsewhere (Ferro 1992) the need to construct a 'place for thinking thoughts' before content can be fully conveyed, and the same applies to dreams.

Violent dreams

For a long time the violent and terrible characters of Giulio's dreams were taken on board, thought of and worked through as if they were mine. He now has a dream in which affective states (peace-loving men with umbrellas) risk being overwhelmed by emotional turbulences (a madman, and children torn to pieces by criminals). He himself says that our attributing these violent characters to my behaviour no longer feels right to him: he now thinks the madman, the fire that burns the children, and the criminals who tear children apart belong to him – he understands that there is a burning personality inside him that sometimes tears his affects to pieces . . .

I am able to tell him that mental health consists not so much in not having these feelings, which must after all be metabolized, as in having a place inside oneself for them: the phobia about what was outside his 'gate' would have no further reason to exist if all these things could now be situated, as in the dream, in his own garden and house.

The cutting off of meanings and the uncle's trophies

After a session in which I gave various interpretations, one of which was 'very deep', Carla brings a long dream, in which she goes to hospital and finds she has forgotten her papers, but her mother brings them. The hospital is a hotel, and then there is a little room where she lies down and her uncle takes advantage of this to cut her hair (cutting off meanings . . . cutting off the flow of thought?). He hangs up the hair together with other trophies . . . plaits . . . hair with a ribbon . . . all this offends her . . . then he takes the lift up to the 116th floor . . . Perhaps a less 'deep' uncle would have done less damage . . .

The abattoir and suffering

Luigi has a dream: he is in charge of a big farm where he has to sort and find places for the incoming animals – bulls, calves, cows, ferocious wild animals, and fantasy animals – which then go to an abattoir, after which they are processed into ham and salami . . . But people too are slaughtered, and this makes him terribly anxious.

He is thus describing not only the work of 'processing' his own primitive mental states, but also the way his 'human' parts are subjected to the same process.

Harpo's harp

Just before the summer holidays, Silvia, now in her fifth year of analysis, launches into a long description that includes stories and feelings relating to an abandonment, accompanied by intense rage and aggression. She also speaks of events from her daily life focusing on her wish for independence and autonomy, and ultimately revealing powerful ambivalence towards her mother, whom she loves, but from whom she would like to emancipate herself.

Feeling that an interpretation about the holidays would be academic and too obvious, I decide that it might be useful to draw attention to Silvia's availability (♀) for taking in and keeping inside her lots of complex feelings at a time, so I say: 'It sounds rather like a harp with many strings, all of which can sound out and be understood.' Silvia's response is ironic: my comment puts her in mind of Harpo Marx: 'That's why he was called Harpo – because, being dumb, he played the harp.'

I feel that this is directed at me, and I point out to Silvia how dissatisfied she is with me for having said so little in response to her material: perhaps her feelings of abandonment, rage, the wish for autonomy, and so on, can be explicitly connected with the forthcoming holidays, as well as with getting in touch with thoughts about the terminability of the analysis.

After a moment's silence, she replies: 'Marisa told me about my cousin Andrea having a homosexual relationship; well, I don't know why, but I am happy for him to be in love and to wait for that person – but *Marisa was over-intrusive and presumed too much intimacy*.'

The first interpretation, which emphasized the presence and availability of the container (♀), was felt to be insufficient, while the explicit second interpretation (♂) was experienced as excessive and over-intimate. In effect there was a container wishing and waiting for contents, in love and interested in the prospect of receiving, but not yet elastic and available enough to be satisfied by receiving a content felt to be too penetrative – rather than the situation described by Silvia on another occasion: 'The feminists say the vagina should wrap itself round the penis instead of the penis penetrating into the vagina . . . even if Elvira Banotti exaggerates somewhat.'[3]

Interpretation and the stitching together of a shared connection

Giorgio brings a dream in which a friend helps him to disinfest his house, which has been invaded by a sea of ants. He is very pleased, and then gives a journalist's sister a manure spreader.

I am very struck, in a negative sense, by what seems to me to be an operation of (ethnic) cleansing, and I interpret along the lines of a process of excessive land improvement that gets rid of everything black and dirty, leaving behind an utterly clean situation that smacks to me of apartheid. Giorgio is manifestly disorientated and anxious, and asks to go to the toilet. After the session, partly because the holidays are approaching and I would rather not place an excessive burden on him while he is by himself, I resolve to return to the subject at a later date.

In the next session he brings a dream: his body is giving off a chemical substance, like phenol, to keep dangerous presences at bay. I ask him if he was worried by what I said to him yesterday and if he thinks he needs to protect himself from other polluting things I might tell him today. Yes, he says, that is precisely what he has been thinking. I now say that we can revisit yesterday's dreams and see if we can interpret them in a way that seems to him more consonant with what he is feeling.

He says he felt yesterday's dreams to be an expression of good and positive things. I suggest that the first dream might also be describing a nice piece of work carried out together, with which he is pleased – a disinfestation operation undertaken with the analysis – while the second dream is about his giving up the 'manure spreader' now that he no longer feels contempt for other people. He accepts this with relief and launches into a long chain of associations about new relationships he is forming at this time.

On the basis of my knowledge of the patient and of the twists and turns of this analysis, I still regard my first interpretation as more *true* (K), but it elicits a 'chemical', archaic, almost autistic defence, whereas the second, although less true, is more syntonic (in 'O') with the patient and *for that reason* more likely to bring about transformations. The second will remain pending in my mind.

6

Delusion and hallucination

Delusion

Delusion is closely connected with *hallucination* (Resnik 1982, 1986; França 1996), which constitutes a massive evacuation of β-elements. Considerable attention has been devoted to the aspect of mental destruction of which hallucinations are a token, but too little to their function of evacuating something that cannot be tolerated, and indeed to the fact that they also have a positive side, in that β-elements can at least thereby be discharged.

I have described elsewhere (Ferro 1993a) the long analysis of a boy who emerged from a situation in which he 'was not awake but also not asleep': as soon as the analysis began, a continuous hallucinatory evacuation commenced, and at least enabled him to be awake. A similarly positive function is in my opinion performed by *dream-like flashes* in waking life, to which I have many times attempted to draw attention.

A similar argument can be applied to *delusion*, the self-containing function of which has been emphasized too seldom. I myself am inclined to liken delusion to phenomena of transformation into hallucinosis. It is something that, instead of being experienced as a dream or fantasy, is projected outside and mistaken for a reality, in so far as what is projected is then assumed to be true.

Delusion is mediated by a *distortion* of what is seen in the outside world, as is graphically illustrated in the session presented here.

Maurizio

Patient I feel awful . . . I wanted to turn back . . . I had a dream: I was with someone who wanted to shove me into a precipice . . . or rather into an unknown world . . . *then I saw a horrible picture, a horrible picture of reality . . . but when I held up an opaque screen in front of it, it looked much more beautiful, less true, but more exciting* . . . then I had these sort of insistent fantasies: Bacon's painting *The Scream of Innocent X*,[1] and then Napoleon and the retreat from Russia – I don't know why . . .

Analyst Perhaps you were so afraid of 'wanting to turn back' to your old ways . . . afraid of the pain and of reality as it is.

Patient Yes, I was very disturbed by yesterday's dream: moving into a smallish apartment, just 60 square metres, with a fireplace and a fridge . . . it really did mean losing everything . . . my grand expectations . . . leaving the palaces behind . . .

Analyst There's also the idea that reality is sad and dismal . . . that it's better to hold up a screen between yourself and reality, a screen that may distort, but seems to make everything look nicer – like the ideas of grandness, wealth and fame . . .

Patient I'm just remembering another bit of a dream: a pig is slaughtered by a butcher . . . then there's a pork products factory . . .

Analyst (I reflect that the first part of the dream resembles the very first dream of Maurizio's analysis – 'A piglet has its throat cut by a butcher' – which I interpreted at the time as his terror of being torn to pieces by my cutting words; it referred back to a sadistic primal scene that had occupied us for a long time. It has now returned, years later, and could be interpreted as the furious rage and desire to kill me aroused by my words. I gave this interpretation when Maurizio began to display a capacity to recognize and contain his own rage . . . but now there is a new element, the 'pork products factory'.) So I say: Now we've had this dream before. I wonder if we can think of it this time as the fear, if you were to give up the opaque screen, of being transformed by me into '*bacon*' or 'salami' . . . into some kind of man . . . if you retreat all the way from Russia . . .

Patient What about the scream . . . ?

Analyst The scream of Innocent X – at this moment too – if the 'Cardinal' feels he is losing the focus of his psychic life . . . you feel that giving up the 'screen' would be a terrible impoverishment, which I want to force you into . . . shoving you into a new and unknown world . . .

Patient I get it . . . I get it . . . The world of people who are all right and productive . . . the world where the plough works the soil.

Analyst The world of work and fertility.

Patient It's agonizing to lose one's illusions . . . the expectations of glory . . . and simply be a doctor . . . being aware of my age . . . of my limits, and working properly. But it's nice not to be a Pharaoh any more . . . and to see that the mind really can be transformed . . . and basically also to think that the analysis can come to an end . . . Yes, I am attracted by that little house . . . it's as if a beautiful woman was waiting for me . . . one I really wanted to get close to.

A few days later:

Patient I feel better today. I feel as if I have a silly sod of a father . . . he doesn't understand anything . . . I've already dreamt of my sister's boyfriend as absolutely indifferent . . . totally uninterested in me . . . like when he was describing a bad-tempered workmate he was talking to about Juventus to keep him quiet . . . and then there was a woman in the birth position who was giving birth to a stillborn baby girl . . . but with her I don't feel any rivalry . . . those are my things . . . it's like the Bermuda triangle . . . I'm captured by it, caught in it . . . either I triumph or I go under.

Analyst I wonder if you might be thinking that things go better when your father is a silly sod . . . or rather when your brother-in-law is indifferent, when you think I'm talking only to keep you quiet, distracting you instead of delving into the roots of your anger . . . and giving birth to things that seem meaningless to you.

Patient Well, yes, but my father isn't always a silly sod: sometimes he seems to say important things, things that strike home and make me afraid, so I feel as if I am in danger.

Analyst I wonder if perhaps there are two ways of seeing me: either I'm a silly sod, and then you're apparently safe, or else I say things that strike home, and then you're in danger – in danger because I can make you see things like the 'Bermuda triangle', or the screen you put between yourself and reality, which may be thrilling and exciting, but shelters you from reality as it is – the reality of a triangle in Val Padana.[2]

Patient Yes, you're right, I love to think about my relations with my father and mother, so as to make up terrible stories about them; I'm transported into this world and am sheltered from illnesses, time and real needs . . . I'm terrified that if you understand this you will take away all the Dostoevsky books and put me in the Piero Chiara book instead[3] . . . and also, if my father is a silly sod, I apparently triumph, but actually I'm ruined.

Analyst The screen is like a miraculous Aladdin's lamp that you only have to stroke to produce exciting and thrilling stories . . . but they deprive you of the world as it is . . . and that only *seems* like a triumph.

Patient But how can I live without the Aladdin's lamp? . . . Today I saw ordinary people in the street . . . how dismal . . . how awful . . . how painful . . . or perhaps I should tell myself that that is real life . . . and that I'm excluding myself from it. What is better, a marvellous plate of food drawn by Salvador Dalí or a common-or-garden meal prepared by my girlfriend when we're hungry?

Analyst And it's that meal you risk losing unless you accept the pain of losing your Aladdin's lamp.

Delusion performs a self-containing, protective function, through projection on to the outside world not of β-elements, which are by their nature unknowable, but of balpha-elements, which are projected like a film that separates, protects – and encloses – the patient inside a 'bubble'; however, although it protects him, it isolates him at the same time.

What is projected inside the bubble, forming its walls, is of course seen as reality,[4] as in the masterly description given in a story by Giorgio Scerbanenco,[5] significantly entitled 'Dreaming to live'.

One of the most painful and upsetting points in an analysis is the *widowhood resulting from the loss of the patient's delusion* – that is, when the patient reacquires the capacity to emerge from the 'delusional bubble' and to contemplate external reality without the interpolation of his own projective stratifications – of those entities that resemble an insufficiently constructed and digested dream (which

I regard as leading a life intermediate between β- and α-elements – that is, balpha-, or β/α-, elements).

As stated, balpha-elements are partially digested β-elements, not yet sufficiently processed to find a place in waking dream thought or in the contact barrier, which are projected on to the outside world and which, as semifinished products, can become linked to each other; they are, quite literally, regurgitations of dream material and are indicative of a ruminative state of the mind. This rumination continues pending a profound restructuring of the α-function, allowing a resumption of the process of elaboration whereby the balpha-elements can be transformed into α-elements.

After many years of analysis, Maurizio emerged once and for all from a severe delusional situation in which he was at first the son of a Pharaoh, then the Pharaoh himself, next a Spanish nobleman, and finally a famous scientist. Emergence from delusion entails a prolonged process of 'catastrophic change' (Resnik 1982, 1986, 1998).

Maurizio went for many years to a psychiatrist who prescribed him massive doses of drugs (in the past, although delusional, he had never needed them), to deaden his intolerable mental pain. Previously, any diminution of his delusions had been followed by characteropathic acting out, which had served as a relief valve for discharging excess β- or balpha-elements. Now, however, although still in a state of anaesthesia or semianaesthesia, Maurizio is confronting the mental pain involved in seeing the world without oneiric interpolations. The loss of the delusion is experienced as so terrible that, after he had come along to a number of sessions with his clothes torn and his trousers and sweater full of holes, I told him that he was like a widower grieving for a beloved companion.

Giorgio

This aspect – that is, how delusion protects and makes one feel better – is illustrated by Giorgio better than by any other patient. Emergence from his state of delusion terrified him for a number of reasons, which he enumerated to me: (a) the discovery that he was mortal, with a finite time to live; (b) the discovery of himself as a person who could fall ill; (c) the discovery of the illusory nature of the objectives he had set himself; and (d) the feeling of being like someone who had to make the journey from 'being Achilles to being a kind of Demetrio Pianelli'.[6]

This journey was accompanied by a large number of dreams. In one of these, the Castle of Fénis fell down;[7] this was his first comment in a dream on the collapse of his delusion and the *invasion of reality*. This is a nodal point of suffering; in other words, there is a reversal of the flow of projections (→) from the stratification of reality by β and balpha to another possibility (←).

The patient recalled Heinrich Mann's novel *The Blue Angel* (1931), and reflected that these new acquisitions meant, for him, that he had to rewrite his entire way of 'being in the world'. However, he was also able to glimpse the first positive fruits of this catastrophe: since he was no longer the centre of everything, he no longer feared, as he had in the past, that if he heard people laughing, they must be laughing about him; he had freed himself from the nightmare of derision.

A second positive point was not long in making its appearance: he was no longer afraid of being a usurper when he began to work, and was no longer the subject of envy, jealousy and revenge, but could plan to help his 'forensic' cousin in the compilation of her many expert reports.

The emphasis now shifted to the fact that the common element in the causes of his suffering was fear, and that he was striving all the time to save himself from a 'terrible, nameless fear' by regarding himself as the 'Prince of Fénis' with the power of life and death over everything. He realized that he had never had 'vaginal' intercourse with the prostitutes he had so long frequented, but only practised sodomy or fellatio. However, this was how he related to the world in the position of the Prince of Fénis: everyone was at his service and under his yoke, and he had never had a relationship of equality with anyone, not even with me in the consulting room.

This realization helped him to become more conscious of the position he adopted in any relationship.

However, if I said anything to him with which he disagreed, he would immediately explode: 'I wish I had a broom to stick up the arse of that disgusting black bastard I saw on the corner': it was the *anger* of the Lord of Fénis that was aroused. What in fact terrified him was his own anger.

Then he was afraid of having caught AIDS and of having no immune defences against the violent emotions that had been kindled, while at the same time realizing how difficult it was to experience a relationship without the absolute immunity enjoyed by the Lord of Fénis.

As stated at the beginning of this chapter, delusion can be regarded as a transformation into hallucinosis (Bion 1965) carried out on reality, which is thus coloured, or tinged, by everything projected on to it and then 'read' by way of the perception of the now polluted reality. This of course places us squarely in Column 2 of Bion's Grid, in the realm of lies and falsehood, but also of protection from something that cannot be tolerated.

Maurizio

In Maurizio's case, what could not be tolerated was the feeling of not being understood or taken into consideration – the fear of counting for nothing – all of which inflicted an intolerable wound that was covered over with the 'keloid' of delusion.

Emergence from the delusion, which had protected him for so long, exposed Maurizio to a minefield of primitive emotions. This world of protoemotions was for Maurizio a terrifying experience; for instance, whenever I said anything that did not correspond precisely to what he felt within, a terrible contempt for me would explode inside him – a contempt which we immediately understood as constituting a 'painkiller' applied to the panic of not being understood and loved. However, the contempt acted like an atomic bomb that razed everything to the ground, thus leaving him alone and terrified. And the same was true of his rage, which was tantamount to homicidal fury – 'I'd like to choke you with my bare hands and then tear you to pieces' – on account of the jealousy and the whole range of possible emotions aroused.

The route to be followed with Maurizio would entail making this volcanic, magmatic world inhabitable, not only working in the direction of its contents (rage, jealousy, contempt, etc.), but also, and in particular, 'imparting' to Maurizio the method (the α-function) of 'working' on these mental states.

Roberta

For Roberta, too, after she had lived in a quite delusional state of 'symbiotic reality', the return to a shared reality was painful in the extreme: 'Reality is like a cold knife blade that tears my flesh apart, and each centimetre of the blade is like an exploding bomb that blows me to pieces.' Reality is what is reconstructed in the transference in the course of a laborious and painful journey, as the patient progressively gives up the erotized aspect of the transference.

However, *transformation into hallucinosis* – that is, projection on to the outside world of something that is then seen as real – need not take the form of out-and-out delusion, but may also assume a more circumscribed guise, as in narcissistic-type pathologies. Here, the most violent emotions, lacking as they do a place for, or way of, being worked on, are projected to the outside and seen there as belonging to others; this process may extend even to the formation of a 'double' (Carels 1998).

However, let us return to Maurizio, whom we left tortured by his widowhood. Faced with new waves of uncontainable pain, he began to 'drug' himself, taking unimaginably high (self-prescribed) doses of psychopharmaceuticals. This was the only way he could achieve the anaesthesia that enabled him to survive. He gradually came to accept that he could recover, at least up to a point, but his life would be marked by years of delusion. He said that his suffering was now due to 'having become aware of "reality", but not yet being capable of handling it emotionally'.

At this point a further necessary but exceedingly painful process of integration began: he had not only to integrate himself into reality, but also to integrate reality into his psychic life – and he had to integrate his own criminal parts, which for a long time had made him want, when he was still a boy, to kill his father and mother, and also to kill his baby brother by giving him 'massive doses of drugs'.

This was what he was doing to himself now: using drugs to blot out the tender, affectionate parts that had begun to come alive inside him, of which he was terrified because they would expose him to the horror of his own fantasies and possibly also to criminal acting out. So, slowly but surely, he began to cut down on the intoxication of the psychopharmaceuticals, discovering to his surprise 'the boy who read poetry', the 'quiet kindness of the newsstand lady' and 'a nice boy' he had met on returning to the lake he had used to visit with his father as a child.

Dreams of sometimes extreme violence – sodomizing the black man with a stick, sodomizing all Albanians, or sodomizing the gardener's daughter (as well as his own needy, tender parts) – alternated with others in which tender, affectionate relations with girls began to appear. At this point he fell fondly in love – platonically – with two women, a 'waitress who gave me milk' and a girl at a motorway service area where he had a 'cappuccino'. If I got unduly close to his criminal aspects, the 'waitress's milk would be scorching hot' and the cups of cappuccino became a scary Capuchin monk or hooded Ku Klux Klan figures threatening him with death.[8]

His tender, affectionate parts gradually gained the upper hand. Although he said he felt normal and cured, there remained a phobic area in his village. He had called himself the Czar of that village, and had drawn up lists of proscribed persons, as well as catalogues of sexual abuses to be perpetrated on the women. A dream put us in touch with 'Ulrich', a Nazi who had escaped after committing atrocities in the concentration camps, and who had to flee to somewhere where he was neither known nor likely to be recognized.

So Maurizio felt safe in crowded places like supermarkets or department stores, which he began to frequent, and where he started to forge relationships that could never get close owing to his fear of being 'recognized'.

He was now beginning to integrate the side of himself that had been represented by 'Pierre Clémenti' in [Buñuel's 1967] film *Belle de Jour* – sadistic and violent aspects – dreaming that his 'sister had pustules', which he described as his own 'antisocial aspects, which disfigure my capacity for affection'. Now, however, the road to integration was open, and Maurizio was able to move through the streets of his village, albeit only in his car. 'Like in a safari park,' he commented with a smile.

Everything else is too recent to be narrated without interference with the 'work in progress'.

Hallucination

Hallucination is actually more serious than delusion. In my view, many phenomena described as hallucinations are in fact 'frames of a waking dream film'. The distinction is fundamental, as it may be likened to the difference between a tumour and an infection – however serious the infection.

Whereas a visual flash is indicative of a sound α-function and an inadequate apparatus for thinking thoughts, 'true hallucination' betrays an extremely severe deficiency of the α-function. I have given a full account of these matters elsewhere (Ferro 1992), and should like here merely to recall the case history, originally presented in more detail, of a preadolescent boy who, at the beginning of his analysis, had 'true hallucinations' involving massive evacuations in bizarre images that lacked a shareable meaning, and suffered from anxieties that were still nameless (β-elements). In the course of these evacuations, which were basically beneficial because they relieved his mind of an unbearable blockage that plunged him into a confused, oneiric mental state, he was totally carried away, as if abducted by what he saw, so that he lost all emotional contact with me. As I gradually became the 'toilet breast' that he had never had sufficiently at his disposal, the 'true hallucinations' came to an end, and were succeeded by large-scale phenomena of *transformation into hallucinosis*, in which he saw the things that he had evacuated massively into me as belonging to me without the slightest shadow of doubt. He discovered a whole series of aspects of myself – behaviours, attitudes, facial expressions, the colour of my clothes – that plainly betrayed, say, my jealousy at the new things that were happening in him; and this, moreover, was incontrovertible. After a long period of work, 'what he saw' began to take on certain characteristics of belonging to his internal world, which he was projecting; he was no longer detached from emotional contact with me, and what he saw was, precisely, the image of a fragment of waking dream thought (α-elements) that was being projected outside himself.

I shall now present a vignette from a stage in this patient's analysis when the visual phenomena had virtually disappeared from the scene and which, notwithstanding my interpretative inadequacies, reveals the existence of a mental container that 'held fast'.

G.L.

For some time, the patient, G.L., had been wondering about the 'class G driving licence'[9] – the *guarigione* [cure] licence – while at the same time he was very afraid of his 'neighbours', who, he feared, were intolerant and might have him thrown out if he was not perfect.

His demand to move into the adults' consulting room was becoming ever more insistent.

By mid-December an absolute catastrophe was already looming, due to the approaching Christmas holiday separation, which he attempted to deal with by resorting to pornographic magazines with sexual images. 'Mummy's going away – who will do the ironing and cleaning and who will feed me?' He kept on insisting on a 'meeting' with his people before the holidays.

Once again he suffered from repeated 'hallucinations', in which he was attacked by *terroni* – southern Italian yokels – who were actually frames from a waking dream film, on which we succeeded in working as if they were dreams. He was suffering from a terrible inner tension that seemed to find an outlet in visual evacuations; this paralysed him and made him feel like 'someone in a wheelchair', and he discovered his need for a mother who was always there (i.e. for an external α-function to help him to metabolize). Terrified and paralysed with fear, he was even more afraid that these feelings might invade and infect me.

To get away from all this, he at times needed to say 'I don't want to come any more', to exhibit rage and to show that he could do perfectly well without me. At other times, however, not coming because of the holidays was feared as if it were the end of the world.

Two kinds of functioning coexisted in the analytic field. On the one hand, he was afraid that the mind of his mother (and of myself as his mother) was clogged up and swamped, taken up with other presences, so that there was no place for him in it. On the other, the mind of his father (and of myself as his father) was organized like his father's shop, on different floors and different levels with separate places for armchairs, living rooms and kitchens. On returning after the holidays, he complained of having been very anxious, even though he had finally accepted his parents' suggestion of visiting his grandparents in France.

As previously agreed, in the third session after the holidays we changed rooms, moving into the adults' consulting room.

He had a whole series of persecutory worries, about presumed dirty tricks by his mother, father and neighbours. He was afraid that I was not understanding anything he was saying to me. He was extremely confused.

At times, after certain interpretations, he would briefly feel 'de-confused'.

He declared himself unable to distinguish between reality and imagination: a 'kind of fog' had built up inside him, and everything seemed 'misted up'.

Gradually, however, he seemed to be starting to find his way about the new room: 'the armchair is made of wood; there's a couch that puts me in mind of "S" [semen], the ceiling is made of cork, and there's a table.' Little by little he was able to metabolize the feelings aroused by the move and by 'not having had the compass of the four sessions' missed during the holidays.

He was often very frightened by what I told him, and was afraid of rebukes and criticism. I felt it necessary not to be in a hurry, and to content myself with proceeding very softly and a little at a time, otherwise he would be afraid that I was 'attacking and destroying' him. Meanwhile, the visual flashes, which had become less frequent since the resumption of sessions, had disappeared completely.

However, I realized the vital importance of exercising extreme caution in my interpretations, and of often confining myself to acting as a 'containing jacket'.

I shall now present some material from this patient's sessions, accompanying it with comments, in italics, reflecting my present standpoint, which differs greatly from my position at the time.

G.L. I've got to go to the barber's today; Anna Rita will be there, but, you know those things that barbers put over your clothes – I'm afraid she won't put them on properly; some barbers fit them properly, but others don't, and then you end up with a mess of hairs all over you.

Analyst You're afraid of getting a careless barber who doesn't pay enough attention to you.

I still think this was a good response: the patient seems to be telling me what it feels like to begin the session by entrusting his head to someone else – someone felt to be receptive, even if he is unsure of how reliable that person is. How will mummy put on his bib? How much trouble will the analyst take to perform metabolizing operations without being careless? Will he succeed in this, or will the patient end up 'in a mess', caused by imprecise interpretations that are too narrow or too broad?

Let us see how the patient responds.

G.L. Yes, up to a point, but I must say the barber is a bit careless about the details: she understands the important things very well and knows exactly how I want my hair to be. I don't know yet what to do about my hat, as it's an intimate thing of my own; so is my jacket, but not so much. Never mind; at home too, I'm afraid of finding the green bedspread soiled with 'S' or that it's been changed.

The patient is broadly satisfied with my responses, but not at all with the details. My response somehow passes muster; its 'cut' was on the mark. The patient now expresses his anxiety about separating from his protective defences – taking off his hat, jacket and bedspread. What is the analyst to do with these? Will he be able to respect them and not change them too much – not get them in a mess for him? But this is not what I had in mind: contaminated by the idea that the patient is telling me about a primal scene, I give him an interpretation which, although unsaturated, he feels to be beside the point.

Analyst It seems to me that you are finding it hard to leave these things alone, to separate from them, and perhaps even more to find them again after you have separated from them, in case they have got messed up, contaminated or even been changed.

He responds to this interpretation as follows:

G.L. Let me tell you something else. In the kitchen too, I'm afraid of making a mess and causing stains with oil, so I have to be very careful. I also have to be very careful when I close the doors of the kitchen cupboard; I'm not sure the door is properly closed, and then I'm afraid to leave go of it – I'm sort of afraid that pieces of the door will stick to my hands.

My view today is that he is beginning to fear that, instead of 'cooking' (with the oil), my words might make a mess and cause stains; the door is of course myself, sitting in front of him – on this occasion we are face to face – and he is afraid he will not be able to prevent himself from being 'soaked' with what I have said to him. I fail to understand this, as my mind is filled with the theory of separation, so I say something that does not fit in with what the patient is thinking:

Analyst I think you're telling me how difficult it is both to be in the kitchen and to go away from the kitchen without worrying: you're afraid of the grease, of getting in a mess, and then of not having closed the doors properly, and of separating in case the pieces of yourself and the other person get mixed up. I also think all these problems apply to *this* kitchen – this room – and to myself as your mother.

His response to this absolute interpretative crescendo of mine is:

G.L. You've really struck home there! I'd like to get myself some gloves, like Claudio's, with studs like nightclub bouncers'; I go dancing at a disco, but in the afternoon there are young people and it's very quiet; goodness knows what happens at nightclubs in the evenings.

He experiences the explicit reference as something that really strikes home, and tells me so hypomanically; he would like to have defences 'with studs on' to get rid of something that does him no good, but instead confuses him, and he cannot understand why a session that began so quietly should turn into something so confusing and chaotic. Absolutely unaware of this level, I defend myself by resorting once again to a saturated theory (separation and the primal scene):

Analyst You come here in the afternoon too and it's a quiet place, but when you close the doors, you are afraid that the kitchen might turn into a nightclub in the dark, and goodness knows what might go on here at night – you're not allowed in, and the bouncer will keep you out.

The patient replies:

G.L. (pointing to an old stethoscope that has been on the bookshelf for ages) What's that? For listening to people's hearts? What do you do with it? I've got a pain here in the nape of my neck, but I don't know what sort of pain it is.

His response to me is: What use is your listening capacity? How do you use it? If you don't use it, you inflict an obscure, unknown pain on me. But, taken up with the (to me!) satisfying theory of separation, I increase the dose:

Analyst If I am listening to your heart, it is because we must part, and we must wait until Thursday to see each other again.

But what happens if too wide a gap opens up between what the patient needs to say and have the analyst listen to, on the one hand, and the analyst's capacity to receive, on the other? What transpires if the analyst's mind is preoccupied with his own theories, so that little space is left for the patient? One session gives us the answer immediately. The patient arrives in a state of uncontainable anxiety, so that the 'analyst's setting has to be breached': the patient's father has to be present at the session to hold back the excess of anxiety generated when the patient feels insufficiently understood and listened to. This session is presented below, together with my curt interpretations, without further comment. What I still believe today is that the setting can be adapted to the patient's needs in extreme situations; after all, so to speak, anything is fair in love and war.

(The patient comes in looking terrified, keeping his distance and remaining on his feet.)

G.L. I feel awful. Can you see? My mother told me something terrible – no, I can't tell you what it was; you can't make me.
Analyst If you feel like it, you'll be able to tell me; it's up to you.
G.L. Well then, I can say it: I had said I desperately needed to let off steam, and she said: 'If you want to let off steam, why don't you go with a prostitute?'

Analyst That doesn't sound to me like something you felt helped by; I wonder if you're thinking not only of something your mother said, but also of something I said yesterday.

G.L. But my mother really did say it, and you said something along those lines too, it's true – but enough of this: I'm afraid it might upset me, so just let me go. After all, my father is angry with me too; my father doesn't understand me, and nor does my mother, and you do a bit, but just a bit – *please* let me go.

Analyst I wonder if you're afraid that what I tell you might make you feel bad – that you'll 'have lost your bolts'.[10]

G.L. Yes, I really am afraid of that – but let me go. Talk to my dad. (He opens the door in great anxiety, and is about to leave.)

Analyst You want to have a 'meeting'?[11]

G.L. Yes, yes.

Analyst But perhaps we could do it right away, and call your father.

G.L. Yes, OK.

(I call the father.) The father sits down; I am in my armchair, while G.L. stands.

G.L. But don't talk to me; you need to explain to my father what is happening.

Analyst I think I can tell you that your worry is that no one – neither your father nor your mother nor myself – understands you.

G.L. We can talk about that, but not about the 'S' – those things are between ourselves.

Analyst Perhaps we can also say you are afraid that Mum and Dad won't allow you to let off steam, but perhaps you're afraid of not being able to let off more steam here, considering that you are in the adults' consulting room.

G.L. That's right. Now I feel 'de-confused', I'm less afraid. I'd like to ask my father something: Will he go for a little walk with me to do some window-shopping before going to work at the office?[12]

Father No problem, of course, G.L., we can do that.

Analyst But perhaps this is your way of asking Dad to be close to you, to show you that he wants to take care of you, and perhaps you are also telling me that I mustn't immediately dive into what you say, but should take a little walk together with you first, to make you feel close to me, and then, once the fear has been overcome, we can work.

G.L. That's right. But enough of that now. I'm afraid. But I don't know whether to talk about it. This business of the bolts.

Analyst Maybe you're afraid that I might babble on at random, and ruin the bit of calm you have achieved, plunging you into *palazzo* – into confusion.

G.L. Here, yes, but I want my father to tell my mother not to get angry, not to go off her head.

Father I'll do what I can, G.L.

Analyst And perhaps you want me – mummy Ferro – to be more careful what I say.

G.L. But Dad, come with me to the young people's shops, the ones with the slightly weird things, the ones that suit me.

Father G.L., no problem.

Analyst And perhaps you're asking me to make sure I can give you 'things that suit you, things that are an exact fit'.

The patient skips the next session but comes along to the one after.

As he comes in he seems to be faintly smiling.

G.L. Are you angry with me?
Analyst Are you afraid I might be because you didn't come yesterday?
G.L. Yes, we tried to come, but the car was snowed in and we couldn't get away; did my father phone to tell you?

A potential short circuit had to be cooled down by skipping the session.

Analyst No he didn't ring, and perhaps that's why you're afraid I might be angry.
G.L. Well, I am a bit, I'd rather he'd told you. Today I feel better; I think I can tell imagination and reality apart better, and I'm not in a dream like the other times. I went with my dad to Via Cavour – there were lots of shops for grown-ups, but none for boys of my age. I don't know where to look – perhaps in the street near the police station, the one that leads from the tunnel.

The 'cooling' has done its job: an effective contact barrier makes waking dream thought readily distinguishable from reality, and the apparatus for thinking thoughts (♀♂ and Ps ↔ D) is working properly.

Analyst I think you are making me see that you're getting your bearings, getting your bearings in Pavia, between imagination and reality, getting your bearings here, and that you'd also like to find things that suit you here, although you're afraid that, in the adults' consulting room, it might be hard for you to find boys' things.
G.L. The main thing is, today I feel 'de-confused', but a bit worried about Saturday and Sunday. Don't say anything, but I went dancing on Sunday and I was afraid: everything got on top of me, and I was afraid of being robbed of all the things I have inside me, my intimate things, money, keys, identity card – but today I feel that the confusion is getting less, and that things are getting back to normal. If you keep quiet, I'll go on.

I'm pleased to have so many jackets, and I think they are starting to suit me again. But one thing frightens me: when I close things, I get worried, because it feels as if I don't really know that the drawer will stay properly closed, so I have to make an effort to be sure.

The patient says he feels 'de-confused', instead of confused as before. What I still fail to understand is the patient's fear of moments when he comes close to me, when we 'dance', and are together, whereas he is less afraid of the days when we don't see each other – or rather, that when we are together I might pollute him, and confuse him with inappropriate interpretative activity. He is still afraid that I might turn his internal world upside down by depriving him of a defensive Gestalt of his that he needs in order to get his bearings. If a patient is at risk of staying imprisoned in the world of dreams, the analyst's interventions must safeguard his 'jackets' and respect his closed drawers, as the most important think to respect is the distinction between external and internal reality, which can be made only if the α-function is not stressed beyond its capacity for metabolization. Otherwise it is like giving chocolate to a diabetic: he immediately falls into a coma due to the accumulation of ketone bodies.

Analyst It's mainly when we are not together that things get on top of you, that you tend to get confused and to lose the things that helped you get your bearings – but you're also afraid that, when I am there, I might confuse you if I say anything disturbing. Perhaps you are beginning to be satisfied again at feeling protected by all those session-jackets.
G.L. But today you seem to me to be right on target with the 'bolts'. My mother is calmer too, and my father said he would go for a little walk with me. Yesterday we were stopped by a policeman, because there was a sign saying we were entering the old town, and then, once we had stopped, we were blocking the way for everyone else.

The last things that were said are fine, but not the policeman who holds up the traffic, as in the first part of the communication. I am again disorienting him with interpretations that are still close to the subject of separation, but irrelevant to what the patient is trying to convey. But, in spite of my inappropriate interventions, G.L. 'holds fast', partly because of my 'civil defence'-type interpretations, and although the session ends with misunderstandings, the jacket-dykes hold firm and the caesura between reality and waking dream thought remains intact.

Analyst The policeman shuts you out of the old town, and we must shut up shop and see each other again on Monday – so everyone is furious.
G.L. Everyone? There's only me. Am I thinking of your other patients . . . !?
Analyst Perhaps I upset you with what I said.
G.L. You did a bit, I thought of the other patients, but then I imagined you were thinking of all the different sides of me.
Analyst But maybe jealousy can make you feel very bad, and cause you to fall apart.
G.L. Yes, but I understood that when you said 'everyone' you meant only me: the foal, the boy G.L., but the foal is not like G.L.'s dog that we talked about before – and then the boy, the foal, is like that man's hat, or his stick – it's always someone with different parts inside him.
Analyst You were afraid I might be looking down on you, but then you got your bearings again and were able to put all the pieces back together, even though it looked for a moment as if they were getting scattered.

7

Characters in literature and in the analyst's consulting room

In this chapter I shall develop some ideas on the concept of the 'character' which I have already discussed, albeit not systematically, in earlier contributions (Ferro 1992, 1993b, 1993c, 1993d, 1994c, 1996a, 1996b); I shall also seek to demonstrate a parallel evolution between the narratological conception of the character (Marrone 1986) and the ways in which it is understood in the various psychoanalytic models.

In his fine short story 'The persons of the tale', Robert Louis Stevenson (1902a: 1) reflects as follows on the status of 'characters' in literature: 'After the 32nd chapter of Treasure Island, two of the puppets strolled out to have a pipe before business should begin again, and met in an open place not far from the story.' This beginning already establishes that the characters exist in their own right independently of the text, with a status that places them outside and alongside the narrative structure, as three-dimensional presences living lives of their own.

There follows a sequence of exchanges between Long John Silver and Captain Smollett, which goes on until, fearing the captain's rage, Silver quickly hides behind his identity as a character: 'I'm on'y a chara'ter in a sea story. I don't really exist' (Stevenson 1902a: 1f.). In this way he both paradoxically and unequivocally demonstrates the reality of his existence. Next comes a discussion about the author and, ultimately, the 'real' existence of characters, beyond the actual paper on which the story is written: 'I can't understand how this story comes about at all, can I? I can't understand how you and I, who don't exist, should get to speaking here, and smoke our pipes for all the world like reality' (ibid.: 4f.).

Doubts are also expressed as to whether the story told in the tale will always remain the same, or whether changes might be possible. In other words, many of the current problems of narratology are stated, although all the implications of the character–author–reader triangle cannot yet emerge. Their emergence may be likened to the transition from plane to solid geometry.

But let us return to Stevenson's tale, in which a clash between virtuous and bad characters is stated to be necessary: 'Now, where would a story go to if there were no virtuous characters?' 'If you go to that,' replied Silver, 'where would a story begin, if there wasn't no villains?' (ibid.: 6). These notions anticipate the work of Propp (1928) and of the structuralists, down to Greimas (1966, 1970), on the need for every 'actor' to have as his counterpart a character who prevents his action.

In the same volume of *Fables*, Stevenson includes a short story entitled 'The reader' (Stevenson 1902b), thus taking the further step that is central to modern narratology, as just stated. Here we have a dialogue between the book and the reader, in which the author is also involved; however, I shall not quote any more from Stevenson, although the *Fables* are certainly worth considering in depth. My reason for citing Stevenson's tale first is to draw attention to the importance that has always attached to the study of characters in literature.

A psychoanalytic session, too, can be imagined as populated with characters, and so indeed it is (except in the extremely primitive situations when the 'character' has to be assembled and constructed in expressible form from highly invasive, dispersed emotional states – Ferro 1998a, 1998b). But what is the significance of these 'characters'?

A little history

In an earlier contribution I wrote that in the Freudian model,

> the characters of the session are understood primarily as knots in a network of historical, factual relationships. Related facts, in this case, are occasions for the expression of feelings, conflict and emotional strategies, which are always connected with those characters. Alternatively, these facts, though considered present and real within the intrapsychic dynamics, may almost acquire an 'autonomous' existence.
>
> (Ferro 1992: 2)

The same situation is in fact reflected in *studies* of literary characters prior to the Propp revolution, when characters were equated in every respect with 'living persons' having well-defined psychological features and character traits.

In the idealistic-romantic approach to narrative texts, then, the 'fabula' is regarded as a faithful reproduction of reality;[1] for this reason, characters are assigned a highly realistic status. Their successful realization and credibility are assessed on the basis of conformity, or a gradient of consistency and mimesis, with the world. The logic of this decoding thus dictates that the attributes of a character and the mutual relations between characters must be studied in accordance with the parameters of reality.

A perspective that is in many respects similar is observed in Marxist and sociological criticism (Lukács 1946, 1948, 1955 and Goldmann 1964 respectively), which studies literary texts as 'significant doubles' of the historical dynamic that underlies them. Characters are seen as representatives, or incarnations, of a contemporary trend (economic, ideological or social, etc.), and therefore as mirrors of all or part of reality (G.L. Barbieri, personal communication, 1998).

To return to psychoanalysis, it is always fascinating to reread passages from Freud's writings, such as the following amusing example from the Addendum to the case history of the Rat Man (Freud 1909: 276): after a *reconstruction* by Freud, or rather after his insistence on the patient's accepting his precise reconstruction of an episode from infancy, the patient responds with a dream in which Professor 'Grünhut' does not spare his 'students' a call on 'drafts payable at a specified place' – demands for payment that cannot be evaded because they are domiciled. Freud of course lacked a model for reading the dream as a response to an interpretation (experienced by the patient as forced on him): nowadays, the 'draft payable at a specified place' would be regarded as an interpretative imposition, and we should have no difficulty in assigning the role of the students to the patient and that of the professor to Freud.

In dreams too, as stated in Chapter 5, Freud (1900, 1914) sought to reconstruct a truth, as in the famous dream of the Wolf Man (see discussion in Bezoari and Ferro 1992a). The patient recalls that it was night and that he was lying in his bed; it was winter, and on the walnut tree outside he could see some white wolves with big tails and their ears pricked like dogs. Terrified of being eaten up by the wolves, he screamed until his nurse came. He was 4 years old at the time of the dream.

Certain elements of the chain of associations are emphasized: the white colour of the wolves; the position of the wolves in the tree; the story of the tailor; the pulling off of the tail of one of the wolves; the fairy tales of Little Red Riding Hood and the Wolf and the Seven Little Goats (the wolf with the paw made white with flour!); the immobility of the wolves; their strained attention; the sudden opening of the window; the wish to receive a double ration of Christmas presents, and the frustration at the few presents he actually got.

As we know, from this material Freud *reconstructs* the *primal scene*: the position of the wolf recalls that of the father in this scene, while the tailless wolf is reminiscent of post-coital emasculation. The dream thus refers to a *real external* event that occurred at a *past historical time*. The key to the dream's interpretation is as follows: the patient unexpectedly woke up and observed parental intercourse *a tergo*; the child was terrified by the father; and the scene was experienced as terribly violent. From this point of view, the hermeneutic end-point is reached when the character to all intents and purposes becomes a person – that is, when the narrative fiction is torn asunder and, as in the well-known story, the king finally appears in the altogether.

In the article mentioned above, Bezoari and I suggested an interpretative approach whereby the dream is read on a different level, without displacing it to another part of the same history, and without referring it to external characters, but instead regarding it as a possible but precise description of the vertex assumed by the patient at the relevant time – of *what* he is experiencing in the consulting room and of *how* he is experiencing it. So it is not necessarily a dream of the patient's history, but can instead be interpreted in the here and now: the patient, lying on his analytic couch at a difficult moment in the relationship, suddenly becomes conscious of a profound inner experience: he is terrified to find himself in the consulting room with the shrewd analyst whose ears are pricked, and sees these ears as beings lying in wait and ready to pounce; his experience is one of persecution, but then he loses contact with these deep emotions and finds himself back in the reality of the analytic scene.

The central issue, then, is the place to be assigned to the primal scene. In the history? In the internal world? Or in the present vicissitudes of the mental relationship between analyst and patient, even if these stem partly from the first two aspects (Nosek 1995)?

However, what status does Freud confer on the characters of the dream? It is a historical, external-referential and symbolic status – but that is not the only possible response. Even if Freud is admittedly performing an extremely modern operation and handing us down a working method through his extraordinary capacity to 'tell a story of the patient's', we disagree with him on the violence with which the patient may experience the analytic relationship in the present. At any rate, though, Freud confers credible, digestible and assimilable form on the patient's terror and panic when he senses the wolf's claws concealed behind the floury-white paw.

The same narrative capacity, or rather the capacity for 'narrative transformation' of emotions, is evident in the dreams presented by Musatti (1949) in his treatise.

The analyst's renarration – from the Freudian perspective – can be regarded as a meta-narration, or a narration on the patient's primary narration, which also contains within itself the interpretative moment, and whose effect for the patient is the more effective the less the gap between the (meta-)narrative level and the critical-interpretative level of the analyst's new text.

This attempt to bring criticism closer to the object of its study, in stylistic as well as other terms, can also be discerned in the field of literature: many pages of Gadda (1958, 1982, 1992) or Calvino (1964, 1979, 1980, 1988) are not mere critical analyses but include in addition a substantial artistic and poetic element. The language of criticism comes to resemble that of the object of its study. One is reminded, too, of *Sogno e poesia* ['Dreams and poetry'] (1995) by the Italian poet Alda Merini, who interprets figurative works of art in poems. From a different but in some respects similar perspective, Barthes (1964) writes that the semiologist is an artist who wants to convey the savour of the signs he studies, and who paints instead of digging (G.L. Barbieri, personal communication, 1998).

Musatti, whom I mentioned above, reports a patient's dream of a barber, which can be summarized as follows: the patient is in front of a mirror . . . he has a cut-throat razor which he does not know how to use . . . he stretches the skin up towards his temples and begins to shave his right cheek . . . but as soon as he starts on the left cheek, the razor slides down to his neck . . . he has a deep cut which is bleeding . . . he takes fright and calls for help . . . the blood gushes forth in torrents . . .

As an exercise, nowadays we could regard this dream as referring to two forms of encounter in the consulting room, one of which proceeds smoothly while the other inflicts deep wounds, perhaps on account of necessary but cutting words, which might make us think about the element of expertise, or its absence, in 'shaving' operations (in relation to the neurotic or psychotic part of the personality – as if the dream included two different vertices?). At any rate, the patient is expressing caution about the relationship and fear of a deep relational encounter owing to its possible consequences.

It is surprising to note that, using the classical rules of dream interpretation, and thus having the patient associate to every narrative subunit – to the narreme rather than the moneme, let us say – Musatti arrives at very similar conclusions, although displaced exclusively from the present transference or field relationship on to the patient's fear of and hostility towards women, and his phobia of marriage, the dangers of sexuality and the wish not to enter into a binding marital union.

In Musatti, the narration does not concern the two minds in the session and the ♀♂ relationship involved in their mating, but is displaced on to external characters. This in fact makes the analyst's interpretation truer and easier to accept for the patient, and is achieved by way of 'free associations' leading from the tragic love of Dante's Paolo and Francesca to stories of throat cutting, of surgical operations, and the like.

Bearing in mind Bion's (1962) concept of 'dream-work-α' that operates during waking life as well as sleep, *I would invert the vertex for reading* the 'free associations': rather than free associations affording an explanation of the manifest text, they are *obligatory associations* that renarrate in a different way the problem of the relational instant, which had already been expressed by the dream and is being retold in different dialects and with a different plot (Bezoari and Ferro 1992a).

At this level a possible parallel between narratology and psychoanalysis may be observed. As we know, narratology sought to identify a schema – a more or less constant structure – beneath the changeable surface of the narrative plot of an individual text. This afforded a fresh view of the romantic idea of the artist's creative freedom, transforming it into the partial handling of a variable quantity of freedom surveyed within a relatively inflexible structure. In a psychoanalytic narration, apart from the binding structure, which may consist, for example, in the fact of belonging to a genre, there is another structure, which is constant although subject to continuous transformation: namely, the dynamic web of the patient–analyst relationship. It is this factor that compels us to reconsider the 'freedom' of the associations considered above (G.L. Barbieri, personal communication, 1998).

It is the emotional climate of the moment that is renarrated by the associations, which draw on the dream being elaborated by the α-function at the specific relational instant – but this in itself seems to us to be a valuable process of narrative transformation and retransformation (Bezoari and Ferro 1992a).

Even recent work by attentive authors of great sensitivity exhibits this predominant approach to characters, which are seen in referential, historical or external terms, and particularly in those of the family romance. From today's vantage point, *I would call this a model based on a strongly realistic reading of communications* rather than a Freudian model.

A fine article by Owen Renik (1998) presents a case history that displays a rare degree of clinical mastery and countertransference sensibility, in which the patient, a doctor, describes how, working in a hospital emergency room, he was able to save the life of a woman patient undergoing a severe hypothyroid crisis. Without going into details about the analyst's working through, his profound capacity to cope with countertransference experiences, and the manner in which he picks up the interaction in the present between his own personal history and that of the patient, I should like only to emphasize that the characters constituted by the 'emergency room', the 'patient' and the 'hypothyroid crisis' are seen by the analyst as 'real' and referential, pertaining to an external event.[2] They are not regarded as emanations of internal objects or of current forms of functioning in the analytic field, in which, say, the patient is indicating that he is capable – even in the absence of a thyroxine function of the analyst – of confronting a severe 'hypothyroid', or comatose, crisis of a part of himself; nor do they relate to other possible interpretations of functioning and dysfunctioning in the analytic field through narrations that are significant in so far as they are events that narrate the field itself.

In the second major model, which I have previously described as *Kleinian*,

> the characters are knots in a network of intrapsychic relationships. Related facts are ultimately a way to communicate the patient's inner reality in disguise, a reality, however, which is seen as already 'given'. It awaits an interpreter to clarify its functioning by discovering its root in the patient's unconscious phantasies.
>
> (Ferro 1992: 2)

An example can be found in a contribution by Heimann (1955), in which a patient begins a session with a great deal of complaining and then fears that he is being persecuted. The interpretation is that the patient's complaining is his way of expressing in the present *his unconscious bodily fantasy* of making a urethral attack with scalding urine, after which he feared the retaliation of the burnt object.

Nowadays I would prefer to call this a *model with a strong fantasy-related stamp that focuses on the patent's internal world* and on its functioning and dysfunctioning. In Segal's contribution on the Kleinian approach in *Models of the Mind* (Rothstein 1985), there are frequent references to the underlying bodily fantasy, which is confirmed as the true 'hero', in the narratological sense of the protagonist with the greatest emotional prominence. From this point of view, the characters of the session appear as susceptible to decoding as, and reduction to, expressions of unconscious fantasies. The fate of an unconscious fantasy is to be put into words in transference interpretations: characters are 'masks' concealing fantasies that belong to the patient and his internal world.

In the field of narratology, an interesting parallel may be drawn between Freudian and Kleinian characters and the entities Hamon (1972: 121f.) calls *personnages-référentiels* and *personnages-embrayeurs* respectively. The former are the historical, mythological, etc., figures that possess so high a coefficient of reality in the narrative text that they appear as actual persons (as in the Freudian approach), whereas the latter are reflections of their originator – tokens that betray the author, his point of view and his ideas (rather as in the Kleinian perspective).

It also seems legitimate to compare the distinction made by Greimas (1966) between 'actors' and 'actants' to the Kleinian distinction between the characters of the patient's narration and the patient's unconscious fantasy (Klein 1929, 1961).[3] For Greimas, an individual character (actor) is the surface manifestation of a deeper, structural and functional dimension (the actant), which, while remaining constant, may assume a variety of external guises; the same is true of Kleinian characters, which can be traced back to an actancy structure that can indeed be identified with the patient's unconscious fantasy. From this point of view, characters are 'doubles' to be reduced to a unity, and they partake of the nature of the shadow in Andersen's eponymous tale (1847), of the many Harry Hallers reflected in the mirror in Hesse's *Steppenwolf* (1927), of Dostoevsky's *The Double* (1846) and of Conrad's *The Secret Sharer* (1910) (Arrigoni and Barbieri 1998).

The characters of the session may prove to be internal objects of the patient projected on to the analyst, who then serves as a screen for these projections and as an interpreter for them on the basis of a highly consistent theory. The need that gradually comes to be felt is not for the construction, together with the patient, of a history, albeit external to the couple, and dating from the past, but for a *code* that can be used with a high degree of generalization (Ferro 1997a).

Abraham (1920: 318) presents a dream of a female patient in which she is sitting in a basket-chair beside a lake in which there are many swimmers, when the arrival of a huge wave and a high wind overwhelms vessels and bathers. Abraham's interpretation of the patient's fantasies has much in common with the Kleinian reading: the wave and the wind represent urethral and anal erotism, while the chair is a water closet.

My own view is that the dream is about the analyst's words, which plunge the patient into a state of confusion. However, the point at issue is not so much the disregarding of a possible relational aspect to the dream as the invoking of partly preconstituted knowledge, which is then found to be present in the dream.

Similarly, in the famous spider dream, Abraham (1922) interprets in a manner that anticipates Klein's part-objects and has to do with the patient's internal reality (De Simone and Fornari 1988).

I have drawn attention in previous contributions (Bezoari and Ferro 1992a; Ferro 1992) to the fascination of Klein's (1961) case history of her patient Richard, which describes a constant counterpoint between what the patient says and the unconscious fantasies derived from it: what the young patient dreams 'means . . .', 'represents . . .', 'is . . .' or 'stands for . . .' – in each case in accordance with a saturated code. Richard's response to these interpretations is interesting: for instance, he mentions 'people travelling in different directions' (Session 48, p. 233) or comments, in relation to Drawing 14: 'This is the worst of all' (p. 215). The bursting pipes featuring in a dream, or boiling water, are read as referring to 'boiling urine', or urethral fantasies, rather than as emotional blockages or signals of the premature forcing of hypersaturated, pressurized contents by the analyst on to the patient. Here again, Richard rejects the drawing.

This kind of interpretation can be found in many Kleinian-inspired developments. For instance, in a richly original article, Norman (1995) reports on a little girl who tells him in a session that she has heard a story about a grizzly bear that was a mummy bear with young; it was a terrible story, in which the mother had a fractured skull and the young bears disappeared. The analyst's response is to interpret the negative transference (how her disappointment with the analyst plunges her into a terrifying world) and the unconscious fantasies about her internal objects. He does not mention the real external world, but instead qualities of the patient's internal world (Uchoa Junqueira 1995): fantasies of a violent primal scene and negative feelings towards the analyst. Nor does the author consider another – intratextual – level that concerns the girl's experience of the analyst's interpretations; in other words, no account is taken of the fact that the narration is also the story of what is co-generated in the field by the analyst–patient encounter. The element of an unforeseeable narration present in Freud seems to have been lost (Bezoari and Ferro 1992a).

It is rather like the distinction between a symbol and an allegory in western culture: the former includes a degree of intuitiveness, openness and unpredictability that is sacrificed in the latter in favour of an inflexible code. The former refers to a mysterious, obscure, contradictory and non-verbalizable reality, while the latter entails the channelling of the obscurity, mystery and contradictoriness into a schema that renders this magma expressible in words. Allegory was the basis of the medieval compilation of encyclopedias such as the *Physiologus*, which contain a coded catalogue of keys for the interpretation of reality (Arrigoni and Barbieri 1998).

In this connection I formerly espoused an *unsaturated relational model* whose roots in my view lay in the work of Madeleine and Willy Baranger and of Bion, and in which 'characters [are presented] as knots in an interpersonal, or rather intergroup, narrative network, which emerge as "holograms" of the current emotional interrelationship between analyst and patient' (Ferro 1992: 2).[4]

In this model, the two minds in the session need to tell, or narrate, to each other what is happening between them, and in particular what is happening deep down in the constitution of a field of projective emotional turbulence. The characters, which will not necessarily be anthropomorphized, permit the coming into being of stories and tales, as developments of the holograms of the protagonists' functioning as a couple. Nowadays I would describe this as a *model with a strongly narrative stamp whereby the fabric of emotions existing in the current field appears as the locus of all the historical and fantasy-related precipitates of both patient and analyst.*

If this change of vertex is considered in accordance with the categories of Roman Jakobson (1963), some interesting observations emerge. In Freudian and Kleinian terms, the *addresser* (the patient) sends a *message* to the *addressee* (the analyst), who performs a predominantly *referential* function in the communicative and interpretative dynamic, his role being concentrated on decoding signs in the direction of reality. All other functions (*emotional*, oriented towards the addresser; *conative*, centred on the addressee; *poetic*, directed towards the message; *metalinguistic*, concerning the code; and *phatic*, based on the channel) are in fact subordinated to the referential function, which consists in the need to seek and interpret the 'real' meaning of the text (G.L. Barbieri, personal communication, 1998).

From a strongly relational perspective, the question arises in different terms, first and foremost because patient and analyst are both simultaneously addressers and addressees, so that the message is structured in accordance with a twofold paternity, which, while as stated recalling a musical score for four hands, is on the other hand also a piece whose author is at one and the same time audience, performer and critic. This means that the five functions mentioned above need not be subordinated to the referential function, which loses its priority, while at the same time its status is transformed so that it absorbs all the other functions. The referential function is productive and useful only if the other functions are regarded as constituent parts of it – the emotional and conative functions (which are interwoven and almost indistinguishable from each other owing to the overlapping roles of the addresser and the addressee), the phatic function (because even contact itself is susceptible to referentialization), and the metalinguistic and poetic functions (because language and text in themselves are not mere materials to be analysed, but essential structural components of referential decoding activity – G.L. Barbieri, personal communication, 1998).

In an analytic session, the same thing happens as in Calvino's novel *If on a Winter's Night a Traveler* (1979), in which not only the reader and the author effectively become characters, but also the narrative dynamic also includes the relations established between the two poles of the narration; in this way, the expectations, questions, hopes and uncertainties of reading (and of writing) constitute the connective tissue of the narration.

That said, psychoanalytic characters take on a particular status. Whereas a literary character is not only a construction present in the narration and endowed with an essential structure of its own, but also a reconstruction by the reader whereby it so to speak becomes actual instead of just potential, the psychoanalytic character lacks a given, objective aspect, because it is articulated progressively by way of the dialogic and projective interaction of patient and analyst: it is a dynamic entity that is never completely defined, of twofold paternity, subject to constant additions and modifications, with a double genetic heritage in a state of constant flux. Even more than in literary narration, characters in psychoanalytic narration prove to be the fundamental element that determines and regulates textual cohesion and coherence, thus making the narration itself legible (G.L. Barbieri, personal communication, 1998).

In this connection, we may invoke the notion of 'interpretative cooperation', initiated by the two poles of the communication during the session in relation to the text that comes into being, as Eco (1979) does in the field of literature.

In Joyce's *Finnegans Wake* (1939), the headland (Howth Head) and the river (the Liffey) assume anthropomorphic characteristics. Then there are the publican Humphrey Chimpden Earwicker and his wife Anna Livia Plurabelle, but unlike the situation in *Ulysses* (1937), these characters do not retain their identities throughout the novel: H.C.E. is also *Here Comes Everybody* – everybody through all time, from Adam to Noah, Cromwell, Caesar, Napoleon, Wellington and an infinite number of other characters of the story and of legend, down to the hod-carrier Tim Finnegan, as well as the common man and the father of humanity (also with the name of Haveth Childers Everywhere). The same applies to Anna Livia.

There is a continuous metamorphosis of characters who transmute from one to another in a history in the throes of constant transformation. This history is seen as the only possible condition for humankind after the 'OK' uttered by the half-asleep Molly Bloom in *Ulysses*, when she accepts the human condition in its historical dimension.

With a view to conveying an infinite range of meanings and a multiplicity of levels of reception, every word in *Finnegans Wake* is a transcription of an ideogram into letters of our alphabet, and what matters is the complex and ambiguous suggestiveness of the resulting web of sound.

Finnegans Wake is the story of a family living in the village of Chapelizod on the outskirts of Dublin, but what counts is *how* it is narrated. The story is pervaded throughout by evasiveness and instability and the narration takes place simultaneously on different levels; the same applies to its language, which is a metalanguage with infinite expressive potential. Similarly, the approach to psychoanalytic narration is based on the criterion of maximum openness, in such a way that the analyst (as well as the patient) allows himself to roam freely between the 'possible worlds' suggested by the emotional context of the moment, at the same time undertaking, outside the text, all the inferential walks that promise to be pleasurable and productive in like measure, without either magnifying or a priori anaesthetizing any possible channel of sense, observing and not creating the successive isotopies called into being by the semantic flow of the text as it forms. Moreover, an important element of this process is the pleasure derived by analyst and patient alike from the interpretative activity: the patent gives up his purely passive role, and participates in the more or less unconscious search for *proportio* that presses for the unification of the words of the text and the elements of reality in an interplay of harmonious relations.

The literary counterpart of the above is the dispute between Rorty (1989), with his reader-oriented, or pragmatic, interpretation, and Umberto Eco (1990). Expressed in the simplest possible terms, Rorty maintains that *any* reading of a literary text is perfectly legitimate because the text is in itself a trace that is completed and brought to life in one way or another. Eco rejects this hypothesis, holding that what matters is less the *intentio lectoris*, as Rorty claims, than the *intentio operis*: the structure of the text includes certain components that sanction a particular reading and stand in the way of another (G.L. Barbieri, personal communication, 1998).

The relational perspective in psychoanalysis places the activity of decoding in an area midway between the positions of Rorty and Eco: the basic assumption is reader-oriented, in the sense that any key may be usable and legitimate, while the emotional and relational context may make Eco's approach more productive, provided that the preferential guidelines for one's own reading are sought in the text and context of the session and not in the analyst's favourite analytic categories.

This situation is also exemplified by Alain Resnais's 'double-barrelled' 1993 film *Smoking/No Smoking*, whose plot is based on a series of narrative forks or bifurcations that dictate the subsequent course of the story: if Character A had done X, so-and-so would have happened, but if he had done Y, the result would have been different. Each branch then splits into two again, in an entertaining interplay of possibilities projected forward into the future and backward into the past. This is certainly more enjoyable on DVD than with an ordinary film shown in the cinema or played back on cassette, as the disc technology allows the viewer to manipulate narrative time in a way that is not possible with traditional unidirectional media.

Another medium that allows one to venture into the logic of possible worlds is the gamebook, which enables readers to choose and construct their own narrative journey and story.

The difference between the handling of possible worlds in literary and in psychoanalytic narration emerges clearly at this point. Openness is essential in both cases, but in the literary field the possible worlds are detours that will be legitimized – or not, as the case may be – by subsequent parts of the text, since the events described have already been written, oriented, structured and finalized. In other words, these are worlds that are 'possible' only for the readers, who are immersed in a textual itinerary that proves to be labyrinthine, mysterious and open only because of their limited and partial knowledge. It is thus basically a question of time, for as the textual journey proceeds, the possibilities and openings are progressively reduced.

In a psychoanalytic narration, on the other hand, the search for possible worlds is a genuine one, in so far as we have a text *in fieri*, constructed by two authors on the basis of a creative dynamic that is stimulating and delicate in equal measure, at the same time rich and uncertain, and, in particular, free of the need to reach a definite narrative finishing line. Here the worlds really are possible, open to a narrative future (the unfolding of the story), but also to a pragmatic present (the interaction of the two subjects in the session) and to a personal past to be made to emerge.

The possible worlds in literature must take account of the concepts of relevance, consistency and legitimacy, whereas their psychoanalytic counterparts are not subject to any such constraints. So 'aberrant decoding' – that is, an approach to a text whereby the addresser's intentions are overturned or at least modified – which is unusual in literature and is accepted only with great caution, is an instrument commonly used in psychoanalysis precisely to make the patient's text say something the patient himself never meant. Psychoanalytic narration is 'used' without the philological, historical, aesthetic and hermeneutic respect demanded by a literary text (G.L. Barbieri, personal communication, 1998).

In a contribution on the thought of Francesco Corrao, Riolo (1997) points out some analogies between the work of the historian and scientist on the one hand and that of the analyst on the other:

> the intangibility of the objective data, the temporal bidirectionality of events, the need for speculative imagination for reconstruction of the text or of the narrative framework and, in particular, the inevitable transformational and distorting interference of the observer with the observed and observable objects.

Riolo adds that, in the view of Corrao, psychoanalysis is not a symbolic system charged 'with deciphering meaning', but a 'system for generating new thoughts' – which in turn 'call for an unsaturated space, a margin of possibilities, an oscillation and a clinamen of sense relative to prior determinations'.

A very important point must now be made. As noted by Mancia (1995), in psychoanalysis a necessary asymmetry results from the analyst's responsibility for the treatment and from his guaranteeing that the transformations that take place in the sessions are – in the language of Bion – from β to α and are directed not towards confirming the analyst's theories but towards making what could not previously be thought thinkable for the patient. The analyst in the session has great ethical responsibility because he is 'treating' a suffering person, and each piece of knowledge accruing on this journey is an instrument of therapeutic change.

I shall now present some clinical examples of this approach, in which the character's reality – both historical and fantasy-related – is deconstructed in favour of its capacity to signify places, nodes or aggregates of meaningful emotions within a field in constant flux. The character becomes the fluid representation in fantasy of emotional and affective colours, of orographic features and of waves of the transformational geography of the field (Bezoari and Ferro 1990a, 1991a, 1991b; Ferro 1994a, 1996a).

Daria's drugs

Because Daria cannot tolerate the 'classical' analytic setting, I have reluctantly decided to accept some correctives that were simply unavoidable. For instance, I allow her sessions to overrun by one or two minutes (or sometimes more); I answer – within limits – questions she asks in the urgency of her panic; I try to replace any missed sessions; and I have given her the key to the street door for use in emergency. All these modifications have formed part of our usual setting for a long time. Now that the analysis has progressed to a certain point, it seems to me that the time has come to discuss these 'expansions' of the setting. I draw attention, too, to another variable that has long gone unmentioned – namely, Daria's need to avoid lying down on the couch, but to remain sitting upright on it like someone surveying the world from a balcony, watching out for and observing every nuance of my facial expression or posture.

After a session in which I attempted to bring up the subject of these 'acquired rights', Daria arrives in a black mood which has not been in evidence for some time; she says she has been to her psychiatrist, who has prescribed 'drugs' for her, which she (the psychiatrist) said were necessary, as well as 'behaviour therapy', and adds that the analysis is of no use, and indeed harmful, for her panic attacks. She tells me I have got everything wrong and emphasizes that the only solutions to her panic fits are 'drugs' and 'behaviour therapy'. In the previous session, Daria said that the purpose of every session was not to conduct analysis but to allow her to leave at the end in the conviction – which had to be renewed each time – that I was fond of her.

Taken aback for a moment and wondering about possible inadequacies of mine, I am able in the next session, when she mentions the psychiatrist again, to tell Daria that she seems to be thinking that 'the panic attacks are something so "specific" that they cannot be made better or treated by psychoanalysis'. Analysis might be fine for other problems. It seems to me that, according to Daria-as-an-expert-on-drugs, the panic attacks can be treated and cured only through *behaviour therapy and drugs* – namely, the key to the street door, my willingness to answer her questions, the tacking on of extra minutes to her sessions, and making up for missed sessions. These drugs and behaviours confirm that I am fond of her, and that is the latest and only treatment for her panic attacks.

Analysis consists of words. Drugs and behaviours are unequivocal facts, which thus have more value: 'So you *are* fond of me *if* you give me the key, *if* you answer my questions, *if* you give me a few extra minutes, *if* you don't make me lose sessions . . .'

Lots of drugs and behaviours are perhaps about to be less in evidence, so what is to be done? Can an analysis be conducted without the 'correctives' of anti-panic drugs and behaviours?

Francesca's cough

In the history of Francesca, a 4-year-old girl, the predominant *character* is a cough – a constant, irritable cough that has now tormented everybody for years on end. The doctors themselves, having failed to find an organic cause despite all their sophisticated examinations, suggested a psychological investigation.

At our first meeting, Francesca's mother tells me that the cough began at the age of 12 months when the family moved and the birth of a little sister drew near. After a few months, tics also appeared: Francesca would breathe in and out in fits and starts.

Recently she has started having nightmares, mentioning 'bad people' on awakening from them in the night.

I think to myself that what was previously expressed by evacuation in her coughing has gradually come to be elaborated into a 'sigh' and has finally become representable in dreams. The mother, however, points out that there is no aggression in her little girl, and that the cough goes away if she takes the drug *Sedocalcio*. This communication confirms to me that the problem has to do with an absent character – namely, the aggression that can be expressed only in symptoms: she can only get better '*se-do-calcio*,'[5] if the aggression is somehow expressed, as in the mother's next communication, in which she says she always gives her daughter her pasta 'with *pesto*'.[6]

The mother has brought along some of Francesca's drawings, which portray a female warrior and a fire-spewing missile.

This initial consultation already indicates which characters might take shape in the place of a symptom that is beginning . . . to speak.

The tangerine and the anti-tetanus injection

A female patient dreams of an intimate situation in which she has pleasurable feelings when I 'touch' her genitals with a tangerine; she is embarrassed and ashamed and feels guilty about the dream. Here there is also a risk of erotization, which can be avoided without hurting her by picking up the positive aspects of this contact – so I tell her: 'It seems to me to be a good sign that there can be a fruitful relationship between us!'

On another occasion she dreams of an expanse of turbid sea with rust-coloured water; as she swims, she also sees some nails . . . she hopes they will not prick her . . . her association is that she has not had an anti-tetanus injection. 'Well,' I comment, 'what you must beware of are those rusty iron [*ferro*] nails . . .'[7] She bursts out laughing!

Characters, as stated earlier, need not thus necessarily be anthropomorphic or animate. The considerations (or 'laws') governing characters also apply to any real or abstract 'thing' that may be connected with the analytic field – for instance, to a 'memory'. A memory as a character of the session can be understood as having to do with the history and thus involving the mnemic function; as relating to a function of the internal world, which involves the internal objects and the relations between them; or as a 'narration of the current field', applying the waking dream thought that is active in the relational field.

Similar considerations apply to the 'history' brought by a patient at the very first interview, and are evident to an even greater extent in supervision groups when the literature of the sessions to be discussed is preceded by an account of the patient's history. This history immediately becomes a character of the field, and can therefore be understood, according to the relevant listening vertex, as (a) a real external history belonging to another place and time; (b) a fantasy about the patient's internal world; or (c) something that tells of the present field of analyst–patient functioning. Item c can of course be expanded to include c_1 if the narration also extends to the group field active at the moment of narration.

8

Notes on acting out, the countertransference and the transgenerational field

Acting out

In considering acting out, I shall for the time being set aside the genetic and intrapsychic aspects and concentrate on the analytic field as the possible *locus* for investigating the inadequacies or failures of 'thinking' – as well as the *locus* for learning, by modifying ourselves and our theories with a view to reconstructing, and sometimes constructing for the first time, a capacity for thought in the patient.

In the therapeutic situation, acting out thus signals an inadequacy of the α-functions of the field (or of the apparatuses for thinking thoughts). While the α-function affected may be that of the patient, it may equally well be that of an analyst who has not been sufficiently capable of accepting and metabolizing β-elements or the patient's projective identifications, or who (by inadequate 'thought' interpretations) has overtaxed the patient's α-function or even – through interpretations which, although the product of fully matured thought, are excessive – the capacity of the patient's apparatus for thinking thoughts.

My thesis is that acting out by the patient is indicative of a dysfunction of the field and hence to some extent also of the analyst's mind. Once acting out (and I use the term to include acting in; where it takes place outside the sessions we learn of it only at second hand) has occurred, it must in my view be considered in terms of projective identifications – remembering that the first signal of a dysfunction of the field is the formation of a β-screen – and hence in its aspect as a communication, of whatever kind (Bion 1962).

Whereas, for example, a dream, thought or fantasy brought by a patient is already rich in α-elements – that is to say, the material has undergone considerable elaboration – a violent projective identification or, *a fortiori*, an instance of acting out is imbued with and made up of masses of β-elements that sorely try our apparatus for thinking thoughts and our α-function in the onerous task of alphabetization, to which we are not always equal; hence the understandable irritation aroused by these manifestations.

I therefore see acting out as a signal of a dysfunction of the field, which, however, contains within itself the possibility of communication if it is received and transformed into thought, however demanding this operation may be (Ferro 1998e).

In Bion's model of the mind, the α-function – so called because we are familiar with some of its factors but not yet with its functioning – continuously transforms all sensory, emotional and perceptual afferences ('β-elements') into α-elements, which are predominantly emotional pictograms that are constantly produced; they are thus mainly visual and constitute the building blocks of thoughts (through unconscious waking thought and oneiric thought).

These operations that lead from β-elements to thoughts are subject to various forms of dysfunction, chief among which are an excess of β-elements and a deficiency of the α-function. In these cases, untransformed quantities of β-elements remain and must take the path of evacuation – through hallucinations, psychosomatic illness or acting out (and sometimes through 'basic-assumption' behaviour). In other words, they lack the 'thickness' of thought.

However, even when everything works and sufficient α-elements, and hence thoughts, are produced, the problems are not at an end, for thoughts, once formed, call for an apparatus suitable for treating and using them (what Bion calls the 'apparatus for thinking thoughts'). When this apparatus is seriously inadequate (it is always to some degree inadequate because, as Bion reminds us, thought is a new aspect of living matter, for which the human species is not yet appropriately equipped), thoughts are treated as β-elements and hence evacuated. (Elements of the apparatus for thinking thoughts are the Ps ↔ D oscillation and the vicissitudes of ♀♂.)

I hold, too, that the patient acts out 'in order not to think'; however, it also a way of expressing a corresponding 'inadequacy of thinking' on the part of the analyst, who may perhaps have given perfect interpretations (which may themselves constitute acting out – see Manfredi Turillazzi 1978), but has not been able sufficiently to accept and transform the patient's emotional state, or to be in unison with him.

This means not that the analyst is to blame, but that he should be aware of the limits of his mind's capacity to receive, to transform and to tune into unknown wavelengths; it is important not to evacuate these limits of the capacity for thought on to the patient alone, but instead to make them the engine of subsequent transformations of technique.

It should be noted that it is not 'the mind' that governs the instincts, and that the specificity of human beings is therefore not a rationality that can control the world of the drives; on the contrary, the problem for humans is the possession of a mind with its particularities. What gives rise to antisocial and violent behaviour is the existence of a mind that has been unable to develop: violence is not a matter of instinct, but results from a suffering mind that disturbs the harmonious behaviour of the human animal – for if human beings did not have minds, they would be functioning primates.

Humankind's problem is the mind and its rudimentary nature – and in particular, the fact that, if it is to work properly, it requires many years of care and attention. A dysfunctioning mind resorts to violence and destruction as the only way of evacuating β-elements.

This is a good starting point for reflections on acting out. A properly functioning mind is one that constantly creates images (α-elements) from proto-emotions and proto-sensations, metabolizing everything it receives and turning it into factors of creativity. It creates oneiric thought, and, from this, dreams and thought proper.

When a mind does not work in accordance with this model of reception, transformation and creation, its functioning is reversed (Ferro 1987; Ferro and Meregnani 1998). What is responsible for this reversal? We already know the answer: an evacuation of β- or balpha-elements. This evacuation can take many paths, including acting out *with* the body (criminality and characteropathy) or acting out *in* the body (psychosomatic illness).

The place of the 'countertransference' in a field theory

When I first started work as an analyst, I saw the countertransference as possessing central and growing importance, and I gradually came to define it in more complex terms, understanding it in different senses and on the basis of different models (Racker 1969; Sandler 1976; Faimberg 1989, 1992; Vallino Macciò 1992; Renik 1993a, 1993b; Ferruta 1998). My interest culminated in an article written together with Francesco Barale on countertransference dreams (Barale and Ferro 1993).

My interest in the countertransference then gradually waned, so that eventually hardly any trace of it remained in my work. Thinking later about the concept, I wondered: 'Why do I seem to know very little, and have nothing to say, about a subject that was so dear to me?' This led me to the realization that the lessening of my preoccupation with the countertransference coincided with my growing interest in field theories: in my view, the greater the complexity and sophistication of these theories, the more marginal the concept of countertransference becomes.

As we know, the first psychoanalytic field theory was put forward by Willy and Madeleine Baranger, two analysts of French origin who settled in Buenos Aires, and can be summarized as follows. From their very first meeting (and even before), analyst and patient form a Gestalt independent of either. In this co-determined field they generate areas of resistance attributable to the couple ('bastions' or 'bulwarks'). The analyst must therefore be capable of distancing himself from these bulwarks, to whose formation he himself has contributed, because, by his 'second look', he can interpret and thus dissolve these areas of intersecting resistance. The entire analytic process is characterized by this continuous sequence: formation of bulwarks, the analyst's second look, interpretation, dissolving of bulwarks, evolution of the field, formation of bulwarks, and so on (Baranger and Baranger 1961–2, 1964, 1969; Baranger et al. 1983).

Various authors (Corrao 1986; Gaburri and Ferro 1988; Bezoari and Ferro 1991b; Barale and Ferro 1992; Ferro 1992, 1996a; Neri 1993) developed these notions into a different concept of the analytic field; having initially been found to be of central importance in group work, they were then transposed also to individual analysis (Corrao 1986, 1987; Riolo 1986, 1989; Neri 1995). This development took place in a climate in which Bion's thought was understood in strongly relational terms.

The *field* thus defined assumes the following characteristics: (a) it becomes the space–time in which the emotional turbulence activated by the analytic encounter is initiated; (b) it is a function of the two members of the couple, as in the work of Baranger and Baranger, but with an extremely high degree of non-saturation; and (c) it becomes the place and time of the promotion of stories and narrations that constitute the alphabetization of the proto-emotions present in the couple.

Transformations of the field are brought about by an ongoing process of co-narration by analyst and patient, who become 'two authors in search of characters' (Ferro 1992), alphabetizing the proto-emotions and enabling them to evolve continuously.

In the *field*, the semantic halo of the concept of interpretation is broadened so as to embrace every unsaturated, conversational intervention by the analyst.

A central element of the field is the *analyst's reverie* (defined as his ability to enter into contact with his waking dream thought and its compositional subunits – the α-elements – and to narrate these in words), which transforms it; however, no less importance attaches to the *narrative derivatives* of the patient's waking dream thought and to the α-elements that make it up.

Considered from a certain vertex, the patient's narration can be seen as a continuous renarration of the way he as it were films, frame by frame, the elements, events and lines of force of the field. From this point of view, nothing the patient says is irrelevant to the field.

The attention formerly devoted to observing the patient's communications and the countertransference now becomes *attention* to the figures that take shape in the field, which emit constant signals of its life. These *signals* must be the starting point for modulations of the analyst's interpretative trim. In other words, all the 'obscure' emotional events that used to be picked up by the countertransference are now *usually – before* activating countertransference manifestations – signalled by the field, provided that the analyst is able to listen to the narrations of the session as forming part of the current field.

I see the field as resembling Escher's lithograph *Relativity*[1] – as a visual vertex – whereas other places in the field contain other possible readings, such as the patient's history or internal world.

According to Bion (1962), a vital function of the β-screen is to generate a countertransference in the analyst when the therapeutic environment is inadequate. It seems to me that massive projective identifications must be activated in order to generate countertransferences. In a properly functioning field, the analyst's attention (attention being one of the components of the α-function) to signals of microdysfunctions of the field prevents the activation of the β-screen, and the analyst becomes the guarantor of the transformational narration – i.e. the narration that transforms the proto-emotions (undigested facts) brought by the patient. In this way, both the field itself and the patient's narrations perform an important function that was previously assigned to the countertransference. The analyst is able to keep watch over the gradients of $\beta \rightarrow \alpha$ transformation occurring in the session.

However, this does not always happen. Instead, we observe *dysfunctions* of the field, in one of which a particular aspect it – the analyst's countertransference – becomes the locus of signalling instead of the field itself. Other possible discharge channels for 'β-screens' are countertransference dreams, acting out by the patient, acting out by the analyst, and psychosomatic manifestations in the patient's or the analyst's body or in the 'body' of the setting. If a signal from the field goes unheeded, it may be transformed into a countertransference manifestation.

In some situations, however, the *countertransference* (or countertransference dreams) assumes great importance as a source of signals – for instance, when the field is 'mute', in an impasse, where the patient obstinately remains silent, or in certain negative therapeutic reactions; in all these cases direct signals from the field are lacking and it becomes essential to resort to this second line of signals (Martín Cabré 1994).

In other words, the countertransference is one of the possible loci of signals from the field, but in this case the field will already be dysfunctional. It is rather like someone at an old-fashioned mechanical typewriter furiously striking the keys at a faster pace than the machine can handle, so that they jam: the typist must stop, disentangle the type bars, and resume work. The countertransference indicates one of the possible loci of 'jamming' of the field – albeit on its margins – which can of course become the starting point for operations of transformation and creation by the couple. In this respect, however, it is neither more nor less important than any other entity that signals a dysfunction of the field and reveals unmetabolized sectors of it that overflow into the analyst.

The countertransference – like a useful episode of indigestion – signals that the field is permeated with β-elements which it has not been possible for the analyst's α-function to transform into α, or his inability to make contact with his own waking dream thought. Working through in the countertransference

(Brenman and Pick 1985) is the method whereby the α-function and Ps ↔ D / ♀♂ are put to work on accumulations of β to be transformed into α, or on narrative derivatives of α.

The present field and the transgenerational field

Transgenerational themes (Faimberg 1988; Kaës et al. 1993; Neri 1993, 1997) are reviewed by Meotti and Meotti (1996). Superimposed on the *present field*, which is *horizontal* and compressed into the here and now, is an equally complex *vertical field* that includes the multigenerational element. These authors thus expand the field and confer the 'third dimension' of height on it; however, if it is considered in terms not of height and thickness but of sequentiality, we also have the fourth dimension of time. Yet this is not a time of 'elsewhere', *but a time that enters into the consulting room.*

We are thus introduced to a geometry not only of the 'internal world' and 'relationship', but also of stories (Barale and Ucelli 1992) and their transmission: instead of the analyst and the patient with two-dimensional 'photographs' of the parents, uncles and aunts or grandparents to be interpreted and revealed in transference interpretations, we have presences and three-dimensional characters of different temporalities, who demand, or need, to take the stage in their own right. In this sense, any interpretation 'in the field' is a transference interpretation.

In my view, in this dimension the analyst must allow himself to be pervaded by such 'freeze-dried' transgenerational elements, which await only the clear water of acceptance of the field in order to be reconstituted and to assume 'thickness' and history.

In the consulting room, a scene is staged and inhabited not only along the axis of space but also along that of time; 'undigested facts' and 'bagfuls of β-elements' admittedly appear in the room, but so do 'packets of α-elements'.

We are thus confronted by a complexity for which we are not equipped; it really is a matter of an 'extempore performance tonight' or, if you will, 'authors in search of characters' – in search of crypts or treasure vaults (Meotti and Meotti 1996).

All this is, incidentally, relevant to the *fascination* of *horror* stories. Stephen King's *Danse Macabre* is an extraordinary history of the horror story, in which it is portrayed as something alien from which we cannot escape. It is my belief that horror, or terror, actually belongs to the unresolved transgenerational sphere that remains alive inside us awaiting narration. Many of the stories of Poe, Lovecraft and King himself can surely be viewed in this light.

However, the field is also a field in the present – for *it is not enough for all this 'to be known'; it must also be transformed* (see the scene from Corto Maltese in Figure 1).

These ideas have many other implications. For example, the narrating function of the field can 'conjugate' the bagfuls of non-thinkability.[2] A number of other points offer food for thought.

First, there is the transgenerational side of the analyst, which also makes its appearance in the room, both as a personal element and *in terms of transmission of the analytic function*, including the analyst's possible blind spots (to which, fortunately, the field can draw attention, if only we will listen to it!). An important issue here is the 'maturation' of the analyst's mind, which is inevitably mediated by imitative identifications.

Second, the history, including our own history as analysts, must be reviewed, not as a rite but as a way of discovering *transgenerational legacies*.

Third, there is much to say about the concept of projective identification and emotional turbulence. A parallel in the world of cinema is the beginning of *Jurassic Park*, where fragments of DNA have persisted into the present. Similarly, the mind can develop only by bringing into the present split-off elements from the past.

Whereas the 'double multipersonality' (Baranger, M. 1959) of analyst and patient previously opened the way to myriads of possible universes along the axis of space, now it inevitably reveals to us a plethora of ramifications in time, or, as Borges (1941a: 77) puts it, this 'web of time – the strands of which approach one another, bifurcate, intersect or ignore each other': the world of uchronias, or utopias in history. So we may consider possibilities that are mere exercises in terms of the history of humankind (what if Custer had won at Little Big Horn . . . ?), but which can become realities in a personal history owing to the phenomenon of *Nachträglichkeit* – for instance, 'If I had not left that trunk in the left-luggage office, how different my life would have been' – and how different that patient's life will be if, together with him, we can discover that laden trunk . . . a trunk laden with . . .

Given the responsibility of parents for their children's mental life, it is possible for anxieties, projective identifications and β-elements to be actively 'injected' into a child's mind, so that the usual direction of flow (from child to parent) is reversed and the child serves as a dumping ground for these entities. However, another situation is equally possible: the parent's capacity to elaborate the child's anxieties may be deficient, so that increasingly undigested accumulations of β- and balpha-elements build up and ultimately persecute the child. Of course, these two possibilities may coexist in varying proportions, and they emerge with great clarity in the field whenever there is a dysfunction of the analyst's mind, either because the analyst evacuates anxieties or because he is unable to absorb them.

Oddly, some analysts say that this 'must' not happen, rather than that it 'ought' not to happen, or that it is desirable for it to happen as rarely as possible. For the analyst's mind cannot but be a 'variable' of the field, since it is not immune, however thoroughly analysed, to the Ps $\leftrightarrow$ D oscillations to which every mind is subject, to mourning and to moments of difficulty, which – unfortunately – will inevitably find their way into the field. This is so although it is the analyst's responsibility to recover his mental equilibrium as quickly as possible.

9

Child and adolescent analysis: similarities and differences that mask an underlying unity

The first issue I wish to address in this chapter is whether major differences that parallel those between child and adolescent analysis (as well as adult analysis) exist between the approaches of the various theoretical models to psychoanalysis (of children, adolescents or adults). One way of investigating the differences between the various models is in terms of the different roles assigned to the 'characters' that appear in a psychoanalytic session. These extend over a continuum ranging from characters seen as possessing 'real external' – i.e. historical – status (father, mother, siblings, friends, sexuality, etc.), via ones deemed to be expressions of the 'internal objects and the associated fantasies', to others regarded as 'expressive modalities of the current functioning' of the analytic couple at work.

In my view, the more analysis is considered as a transformational interaction between analyst and patient in the present, the more age-related differences between patients are blurred and the more significant the specificities of the particular analytic couple become. The more the characteristics are considered in terms of age and behaviour ranges, these being correlated with developmental stages and fantasies attributed to the patient, the more differences will be discovered (Marcus 1980; Bernstein 1975).

My personal conviction is that there exists a *unity of transformations and analytic interaction and a specificity of expressive forms of language*. For instance, many adult analysts claim to feel closer to, and find it easier to approach, adolescent analysis owing to their avowed concern with the different forms of expression (play, drawing, acting out in the session); one may, however, suspect that they are in fact preoccupied with the 'infantile' (Guignard 1996). Many analysts would agree that adolescent and infantile aspects are encountered in any analysis, including those of adults (Aalberg 1997), and that the adolescent and infantile aspects of the analyst are also activated.

How does an analysis work?

This may seem a naive and superfluous question, since, of course, we all know the answer. However, I should like to explain what I mean by the unity of analytic processes by telling the story of a film and then reporting an analytic session.

Jumanji

Joe Johnston's 1995 film *Jumanji* is based on a novel by Chris Van Allsburg. One day at an archaeological dig, a little boy, Alan Parrish, finds a box containing a board game with a kind of central lens in the board and a number of pieces. After a row with his father, he and a little friend, Sarah, begin to play. Sarah rolls the dice, a particular number comes up, and out of the lens come a vast swarm of bats that invade the room. Then, when it is Alan's turn, the lens sucks him through the board into a jungle, where he must remain until another player throws a certain number – but his little companion runs away in terror, breaking off the game.

The scene changes to a time 26 years later: the Parrishes' house is for sale, the owners having died in misery after spending all their time and money in a futile search for their son following his mysterious disappearance.

New people move into the house: Peter and Judy, a brother and sister orphaned after losing their parents in a car accident, together with their aunt. Up in the attic one day, they happen upon the box with the game. They open it and begin to play. Once again, terrible things emerge from the central lens: enormous mosquitoes, which first invade the room, then the whole town . . . and so on. Eventually, as they play, the dice come up with precisely the number that would have allowed Alan to return in the original game – and that is precisely what happens: on to the scene steps Alan, 26 years older, dressed like a denizen of the jungle . . . and pursued by a lion. After a series of mistakes and terrifying vicissitudes, Alan and the two children realize that, to continue, they must find the little girl from the original game, as the pieces have to be moved in a precise sequence and the others cannot be moved unless Sarah joins in.

The three go in search of Sarah, whom they find grown up – 26 years having of course elapsed! – and working as a medium. We later discover that she has undergone prolonged psychotherapy to persuade herself that what she experienced never happened – namely, that bats came out of a board game and that Alan was sucked into it and disappeared.

I omitted to mention that the reason why the game had to be resumed was that, according to one of its rules, all its effects would come to an end only *if* and *when* it was brought to a conclusion.

Sarah is persuaded to play again. Further terrible things happen in the playroom and spread to the town: plants with roots that grow so stupendously fast that they penetrate and destroy everything in their path; headlong charges by rhinoceroses, elephants and other jungle animals; a hunter, also from the jungle, with the same features as Alan's father, who wants to kill Alan; and, for good measure, monkeys that invade the town and cause mayhem, alligators, floods and every kind of calamity.

All these vicissitudes are interspersed with constant incidents whereby the game risks being carried away either by the hunter or by flood waters, in which case it would never reach its conclusion and all the terrible events would never be undone.

But in the end Alan somehow manages to throw the number that takes him to the home square, and to pronounce the fateful word: 'Jumanji'. Then the miracle happens: everything that had come out of the lens spirals back into it – the bats, the mosquitoes, the monkeys, the hunter, the rhinoceroses and the elephants, which are sucked 'backwards' from outside to inside by a kind of tornado. All the effects of the game are undone – and I mean *all* of them: Alan is back in the room as a little boy with Sarah as a little girl; the other two children are not there because we have gone back 26 years and they have not yet been born!

From then on, we have a different reality from the one that existed from the time of Alan's disappearance on. Alan's father comes home and his son embraces him; the story is rewritten from this point on without all the catastrophes of the previous script.

The Parrishes' shoemaking business does not fail; Alan becomes its owner and marries Sarah when they grow up. However, they have not lost the memory of the other story, and when, 25 years later, they meet the two children Peter and Judy at a party, they immediately recognize them. When they hear that the children's parents are about to leave for Canada, they manage to stop them, so that they do not die and leave their two children orphaned. At the end of the film, other people seem to retrieve the 'game', which Alan had consigned to the waters to get rid of it . . . and so the game continues.

There are of course an infinite number of possible readings of this 'story', and no limit to the drift of meanings and possible deconstructions. This is so even if we confine ourselves to a single vertex, namely that of psychoanalysis: here alone, we could range between the surname of the hero, Parrish, which may suggest 'parricide', the resulting persecution, the reconciliation that tells a different story from that of the 'orphaned children', and other possible content-related and symbolic readings.

However, my preferred 'invention' (or 'selected fact' – Bion 1963 – on the basis of an emotion that assembles the facts into a possible Gestalt) is to see the events described in the film as a thoroughly apt metaphor of the analytic encounter – as a game that can be played by the adult, adolescent and infantile parts of both analyst and patient. What come into being in this game are the emotions, affects and characters that narrate and personify it, invading the room, the setting and the internal world (and sometimes the external world too) through constant externalizations (transformation into hallucinosis, hallucinations and evacuations) that activate imitative fury, rage, persecution and fetal fantasies; yet, in spite of all the difficulties, the game *must* be brought to a conclusion, because it is only then that the inversion of the inverted α-function (Bion 1962) – i.e. the metabolization of previously acted-out fantasies – will put things back in their place, so that what had been evacuated can be transformed and reintrojected (i.e. made thinkable).

All this, however, permits the complete rewriting of the patient's history, not only in the present but also transgenerationally, so that the transformed proto-emotions can return and inhabit an unconscious that is now sharply distinguished from the waking world, which need no longer suffer its encroachments.

This, in my view, is the game of analysis: getting in touch with the entire unthinkable and unrepresentable world that was previously throbbing away amorphously, so as to confer on it a representation capable of 'narration', after which it will be able to reinhabit an unconscious composed now of narratable, albeit repressed, elements of a story. In other words, the throbbing mass, or accumulation of β-elements, is first evacuated, elaborated and transformed into α, and can only then be reintrojected as a dream of the mind about itself ('waking dream thought' and 'thoughts' – see Bion 1962, 1963, 1965).

Moreover, the 'central lens', which produces lines of verse before its projected outpourings, is like an analysis that can accommodate the most violent emotional turbulence, where projective identifications find a space in which they can be received and where no attempt is made to avoid the transformations into hallucinosis that may arise in the field – let alone the hallucinations, acting out and other manifestations entailed by the free, turbulent circulation of β-elements, which must of course find their way into the field as a prerequisite for transformation.

This means that a board lacking a central 'lens' capable of dreaming and evacuating permits only those more classical games that do not afford access to the more primitive jungle which lies beyond the repressed – i.e. β-elements.

Again, when the little girl drops out of the game, we can see this as an attempt to escape from the involvement of her infantile parts, resulting in an impasse and intense negative transference; these are later metabolized by the restoration of genuine cooperation between the adult, child and adolescent aspects of both patient and analyst, which must necessarily all be present together in the analytic field.

How do adults, adolescents and children coexist in the consulting room in an adult analysis?

The Russian doll: the adult, the child and the adolescent

Giorgio, an *adult* analysand, begins a session in December by telling me about a severely depressed man undergoing treatment at a psychiatric unit: when his landlady breaks an unspoken agreement by demanding a rent increase, he immediately shoots both the landlady and himself dead.

For some time I have been wondering whether it might be appropriate and possible to ask this patient for an increase in the fee for his analysis from January, and have decided, for a number of reasons, not to do so. I therefore reply: 'Well then, thank goodness *I* didn't ask you for an increase in the New Year!' After a moment's surprised silence, the initially disconcerted Giorgio bursts out laughing.

The patient misses his next session, and in the one after that he tells me how his *16-year-old daughter* has resumed their previous warm and playful relationship, 'giving him a friendly punch in the stomach' when passing in the corridor; although this pleased him, he did not come because his *8-year-old son* was struck violently by a ball while playing with his mates and sustained severe bruising, so that he had to be kept at home from school for a day.

Although I do not say so, I of course see the missed session and what Giorgio tells me as the response of his *adult*, *adolescent* and *infantile parts* to my interpretation, which he no doubt felt as a blow: he had to miss the session although he had rediscovered a warm relationship with me, because the warmth wounded him, mortifying his most fragile parts.

Let us consider the characters involved: *Giorgio*, the patient, a 50-year-old lawyer of Latin American origin; *Carla*, the rebellious 16-year-old adolescent daughter who doesn't speak if she is angry, doesn't go to school and doesn't do her homework; and *Stefano*, the 8-year-old son, a delicate boy whose joints are easily damaged. How are we to think of these characters on the analytic stage?

From a certain vertex, they are of course real persons: the father, the daughter and the son. From another standpoint, however, Carla and Stefano are also Giorgio's internal objects. Obviously, too, considered in still other terms, they have to do with current modes of functioning of our relationship in the analytic consulting room.

I found it very difficult to discover appropriate modes of interpretation with Giorgio; at first I thought I could interpret his communications exhaustively and directly in the transference, but then sessions would be missed, dreams would be forgotten (Carla) and the work would grind to a halt (Stefano).

Eventually, however, I succeeded in distinguishing between these three forms of functioning in the room, each of which called for a different interpretative strategy. With 'Stefano', it was vital for me not to say anything that he would experience as intrusive or in any way 'wounding'; I needed to interpret in narrative form, in images and metaphors, as if playing with words until a shareable meaning could be constructed. With 'Carla', I had to 'accept and gently transform', as if dealing with a hedgehog, avoiding any direct, explicit and immediate interpretation in the transference. With Giorgio, it might be permissible to interpret by talking about characteristics of 'Stefano', who bled if he were hit, or 'Carla', who played truant if . . . or would not speak if . . .

Giorgio is gradually becoming able to integrate these things, which are narrated like a story about Carla or Stefano – and, albeit at an incredibly slow pace, is taking them on board as his own.

However, what does all this mean? In a sense, it is indeed true that the adult, the adolescent and the child are always present in the analyst's consulting room. Of course, an infinite number of combinations are possible.

The adolescent and the little girl

Silvana suffered a severe trauma at the age of 4, after which she lost the faculty of speech for a long time, but gradually regained it. She is now an intelligent, alert teenager currently having inexplicable difficulties at school, which I felt to be related to the traumatic experience and to anxieties that seemed beyond my reach until the drawings Silvana has begun to make in her sessions made it possible to delve into the quality of our communication. One of these (Figure 12) shows two music stands with books; the one on the first stand is on fire and, to save his life, one of its characters leaps into the other book. He greatly misses his companions from the first book, and has to confront new stories and situations in the second.

With the gradual emergence of these stories, Silvana draws a faceless figure (Figure 13); next comes a face, part of which is 'protected by an iron cap' (Figure 14), but which begins to reveal itself as an unknown and enigmatic aspect about which questions can be asked (Figure 15). Eventually, further transformations lead to a masked face (Figure 16) and then a skiing outfit with goggles that disclose '90% of what is inside' (Figure 17).

So I find myself with an adolescent containing a little girl who does not speak but is increasingly capable of expressing herself through drawings.

At this point, however, a further question arises: what changes if we have in the consulting room not infantile or adolescent 'aspects' or 'parts', *but actual children and adolescents*, as Mächtlinger (1987) points out? Furthermore, what formal and, in particular, substantive differences are there between child and adolescent analysis?

Formal similarities and differences

For reasons of space, I shall not dwell on the obvious formal differences. A child plays, draws and 'moves about' in the consulting room, while the analyst for his part is 'dragged' into these activities (Ferro 1995c, 1996g, 1997b; Sacco 1995a, 1995b). An adolescent, on the other hand, does not usually play or draw, and stays relatively still.

However, these differences are not absolute (Markman 1997; Ferro 1996e). A 16-year-old girl who finds it hard to get in touch with things that lie deeply

Figure 12 From the old story to the new

buried beneath her ritual communications about her 'studies' takes a calculator from her rucksack, tries to open it up, succeeds in doing so, looks inside and says: 'How ugly the inside of a calculator is.' This immediately re-establishes our communication: I am able to tell her (for she can accept and use clear, explicit interpretations) that she is afraid of revealing ugly aspects of herself, connected with her fear of being a 'calculator' or profiteer . . . and this fear makes her keep everything 'locked up inside'.

However, an adolescent too, as in the case of Silvana – and why not also an adult? – can draw in an analytic session (Decobert and Sacco 1995). An example is Martina, an adult patient, who, to show me what happens if anything sounds to her like a criticism or if she thinks she has criticized me, draws two cats tearing each other to pieces and furiously gobbling each other up, leaving only a tail: end of story.

Figure 13 Silvana's unknown face

Not only adolescents but also adults may act out in an analytic session; such instances can be seen not merely as an attack on the setting, but also as a communication. I recall one patient who came into the room, ensconced herself on my writing desk and refused to budge until I told her that she reminded me of Calvino's 'Baron in the Trees', who was so offended by his fellow-men that he no longer wished to share the earth with them and decided to take refuge in the treetops; this enabled me to link the patient's indignant reaction to what had happened in the previous session.

Adolescents certainly tend to act out; Ladame (1980, 1992) draws attention to the communicative aspect of these situations, which resemble dream scenes. However, children and many adult patients with evacuative tendencies also act out.

Figure 14 The protective cap

Figure 15 The enigma and curiosity

Although reporting dreams or narrating events from daily life is more common in adolescents, children may do so too. I have always felt it important and moving when, in working with a child on the threshold of adolescence, we start thinking about transferring to 'the adults' consulting room', which I also use for adolescents.

This decision will have called for a change in the style of communication: play, drawing and movement will have increasingly given way to verbal exchanges. It seems to me that the more 'languages' and linguistic registers the analyst is familiar with, the more this change will be facilitated (Amati Mehler et al. 1990). Everyone working not only with children and adolescents but also with seriously ill patients who often resort to such means of expression knows this: for instance, a psychotic patient responded to an interpretation of mine that displeased him by taking off one of his shoes, sniffing it and declaring contemptuously: 'Plastic!'

However, this quite explicit level is surely less interesting than the deeper problem of *substantive* similarities and differences – i.e. ones that concern theory, the theory of technique, and technique itself (Olmos de Paz 1996, 1998).

Substantive similarities and differences

The analyst's models

On this level, a very important factor, to my mind, is *the analyst's theoretical model*; as stated at the beginning, a very simple and clear key to the relevant models is

Figure 16 Now it's only a mask

Figure 17 I'm 90% sure who I am

the analyst's approach to the characters that come to life in the sessions (Ferro 1993c, 1996e).

Interpretation

Rather than wonder about the age of the person to whom an interpretation is directed, I ask myself about that person's capacity to accept the interpretation, as constantly signalled to me by the responses to my interventions. It is also, in my view, important to respect the patient's text for long periods without excessive interpretative caesuras. I believe, too, that, with adolescents and adults, we can learn to interpret 'as if playing' or 'as if drawing' – that is, as if using words as a drawing that changes or is enriched or coloured in various ways.

Another important element is the transformation achieved, which does not solely and necessarily involve the disclosure of something, but also entails constant elaboration of the emotions present in the session, so as to unfreeze the 'frozen game' represented by every symptom. A similar view is taken by Gibeault (1991), who, citing Berberich (1990), distinguishes interpretation *in* the transference from interpretation *of* the transference.

These matters are thoroughly discussed by Bonaminio (1993), Bezoari and Ferro (1989, 1994a, 1994b), Fonagy and Sandler (1995) and Norman (1995), and are central to Guignard's (1998) article.

The countertransference

This may be the level of the most significant differences. There are in my view periods in an analyst's life when he prefers to have child or adolescent patients. Colleagues I have asked about this point report a wide variety of individual experience.

Working with small children is more tiring – if only, according to some, in motor terms. Many who have treated young children switch at some point to supervision of such treatments: Waksman (1985) and Siniavsky (1980) emphasize the greater level of mental fatigue, the difficulty of grappling with archaic identifications, and the need for – sometimes even physical – containment.

What matters most is often held to be the analyst's internal cohesion in relation to the analytic situation – that is, the analyst's internal setting or, in other words, the internal situation from which he interprets. This is surely the main point made by Laufer (1997, 1998), who has often drawn attention to the importance of the analyst's 'scotomas', which are substantially analogous to Guignard's (1998) 'blind spots'. It is impossible to disagree with Laufer's view of the fundamental need for a deep understanding of our adolescence and its continued role in adult life. In this author's opinion, in the analysis of analysts-to-be, infancy is as a rule examined in some depth, while adolescence is neglected. Yet, he goes on, it is essential for the future analyst (of adolescents?) to be capable, in his own analysis, of assigning not a theoretical but an affective reality to his own adolescence: he must have been able to summon up and reconstruct the fantasies, fears and perverse and psychotic acts of that age, the moments of loss of control, and the sense of his own sexual and masturbatory practices.

The analyst (perhaps of adolescents) must be equipped to work with virtual psychotics and have worked through his psychotic defences; he needs great internal freedom if he is to be able to say (and tell himself) everything, whether it be homosexual fantasies and attractions or violence – for psychotic nuclei must be confronted in order to work through them (Olmos de Paz 1990).

Cahn (1997), too, draws attention to aspects of the countertransference – in particular, feelings of longing or the anxiety-related avoidance of excitation, agitation, confusion and the alternation of despair and hallucination. Owing to the difficulties of relating to adolescents, Anderson (1997) advocates specialization, following prior experience with either adults or children. However, it is interesting to note that Guignard, whose 1987 article is devoted precisely to the similarities and differences between child, adolescent and adult analysis, emphasizes the countertransference effort required with children and the difficulty of maintaining an analytic position owing to their motor discharges.

The setting

The first problem arising is that of session *frequency*, on which a wide variety of opinions have been expressed (Anderson 1993; Berberich 1993; De Levita 1993; Schacht 1995). This question must therefore remain open.

Another important factor is of course the differing weight assigned to the *presence of the parents and the relationship/vicissitudes with them* (Norman 1993; Eskelinen de Folch 1988). Laufer (1998) gives a particularly clear account of this issue. My own attitude towards parents has gradually mellowed and become more accepting, as I have progressively tried to adopt a more constructive approach. I do not refuse meetings when requested, and as far as possible I regard parents as allies (even if they have sometimes unconsciously sabotaged the work). An idea I have found useful in this connection is Kancyper's (1997) extension of the concept of the field to the entire analytic situation with children and adolescents, including the relationship with the parents (Goijman and Kancyper 1998).

Furthermore, I proceed in the same way with the parents or relatives of psychotic analysands, whom I try to refer to a colleague, but for whom I try to be accessible whenever I am asked and I consider it useful. Eskelinen de Folch (1988) discusses this issue at length, together with its countertransference implications.

What I have felt to be most important is the need to respect the confidentiality of adolescent patients who place themselves in risk situations: their communications, after all, were made in a setting that presupposes secrecy.

Narrative scenarios and their characters

The scenarios encountered in child analysis are usually less realistic and more fantastic – full of animals, witches and ogres – than those of adolescents. However, in my view, for all the manifest differences, there are substantive similarities.

I give my students what I believe to be a useful exercise, asking them to consider how one and the same theme might be expressed by a child, an adolescent and an adult. This involves taking a real session with a child and rewriting it in the form it might have assumed with an adult patient, and then taking a real session with an adult and rewriting it with the expressive modalities of a child. I have seldom encountered material so specific that it does not point to something deeper than the manifest aspect, which could not be expressed in adult, child or adolescent language.

It seems to me that what changes is the plot, but not the fabula[1] – the 'plot' being the story as told, as it appears on the surface, and the 'fabula' the fundamental pattern of the narration, the syntax of the characters, and the profound mental exchanges between patient and analyst.

10

Play: characters, narrations and interpretations

This chapter is intended as a reflection on how best to approach patients and on how to encourage trust and hope in the analytic encounter. It deals with the effects of interpretation and the way the characters and narrations of the sessions provide us with extremely valuable signals that enable us to modulate our interventions. This presupposes that characters and narrations are regarded as events of the relational here and now and not merely as derivatives of the individual patient's history and internal world.

Let me begin with a play sequence from a child analysis, as a basis for the development of theoretical observations. The clinical material dates back many years, so that I can clearly see how my ideas have changed over time; I find it painful to look back in this way, in view of everything I failed to understand despite the patient's indications.

Massimo

Massimo is a 9-year-old boy who has been brought to analysis on account of serious problems at school: his academic performance is excellent, but his relations with his schoolmates are very bad. He has been tortured since birth by regularly repeated surgical *interventions* for certain malformations (plastic surgery). He also suffers from serious anorexia; he eats little, always consuming minimal amounts of the same foods, intellectualizes constantly and is remote from his emotions. The following sequence of sessions chosen at random from the first year of Massimo's analysis illustrates some problems of technique.

Monday

Massimo begins by taking some wooden blocks from the toy box and starts making a figure of a man (a), followed by that of a boy (b).

(a)

(b)

While making the figure of the boy, he comments that, if the boy's head is to stay in place, it needs to be supported by something, so he puts the locomotive – 'it's made of iron,[1] so it's strong' – behind it, but says we are not to think about it.

I now point out to him that, here in the room, there are also a man and a boy, and that the boy needs to have his head supported – by the locomotive, which is made of iron [*ferro*], just as he needs to be supported by Dr Ferro. *(After Massimo's first communication, I immediately give a transference interpretation, but from today's vantage point I feel that it prematurely closes off and saturates what is happening; nor do I respect Massimo's need for the support to remain implicit ['We mustn't think about it']. Today, I would give a more open, less saturated intervention, perhaps asking a question about the boy's head.) However, let us consider the response to my strong, univocal entry on to the stage.*

He says: 'I see what you mean about the boy needing help.' He now starts 'making an animal', putting its legs obliquely under a rectangle as if it were in motion – 'an animal running away, or escaping' (c).

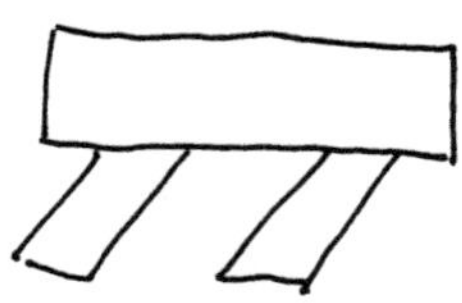

(c)

The figure's balance is precarious, and the whole thing collapses when he adds further pieces, until he makes the animal's legs upright (d).

(d)

He now finishes off the construction, which reveals itself as a cat (e).

(e)

He tells me it is a cat, an animal he is very fond of. *The verbal response is conciliatory. Today I tend to see the 'animal running away, or escaping' as Massimo's deep emotional reaction to my first interpretation, which generates 'panic' and then humiliation – everything collapses – until the flight is at an end (he gives the animal upright legs). He now produces the cat, which today suggests to me distrust and suspicion. (This character, who is 'born' at this point in the session, can be seen as something that has to do with Massimo's real external experience, with distrust in his relationship with his parents, or with an internal object attributed to the boy; however, it can also be regarded as something that comes to life in the room through the interaction between our minds: the way I interpreted generated fear, disappointment and flight in the patient, all of which flow into the cat, who represents the affective quality of the moment. Although I did not then think in these terms, I am obviously cautious nevertheless.)*

I ask him what aspects of the cat he likes, and he answers: 'Cats are crafty; they don't trust anyone and they're suspicious.'

(Massimo puts into words the view I would take today of the quality of the emotional field that has formed.)

I tell him that he wants to talk about feelings like that towards me, that he feels suspicious and distrustful, and wonders if he can tell me the things he is thinking or if it would be wiser for him to keep them to himself. I pick up the last drawing from the previous session, which is lying on top of the other drawings and represents a road roller, and suggest that what happens between us might be like the interaction of a roller and stones. *(Here again I felt the need to give a transference interpretation, interpreting the cat as something belonging to him and not as an entity partly generated by my first interpretation. I then have a reverie – although I did not realize it at the time – and use the drawing from the previous session to tell him (quite unconsciously) what has been happening: I was squashing him with my knowledge about him, like a road roller, rather than helping him to develop thoughts with my help.)*

He says everything I am telling him might well be right, although he doesn't feel that he thought it himself.

Tuesday

In the next session, Massimo is very quiet and sullen; he decides to make a drawing from the three-dimensional figure of the cat 'so that I can redo it whenever I want'. He then begins to number the drawing sheets, a process that takes a long time. I tell him that he wants to keep everything well classified and to see if I too remember the order of the work we are doing. He then invents a complicated key to his sheets of drawings.

I tell him he wants 'to be sure that he can keep everything under control'. *(Today, it seems to me that the effect of my interpretations of the previous day has been to make him sullen and sad, and that the effect of my oversaturated interpretative activity has squashed him, flattening out the cat and our communication. I interpret academically, thus stripping the session of affect.)*

Wednesday

On arriving for his next session, Massimo takes off his coat, which falls to the ground. He comments: 'My coat slipped off because it's heavy and the lining is smooth.' He goes on: 'Let's make some more animals with the blocks.' He takes the blocks and builds a very realistic, very big dog; he wants to draw it too on a sheet of paper, but one sheet is not big enough; he asks me if I have some glue to stick several sheets together, and I say I will get some for next time. He says: 'But I can try to make some other animal – say, a rabbit.' I watch in astonishment as a rabbit comes into being before my eyes; he has difficulty in shaping the head.

I ask him what these animals suggest to him, and he replies: 'The cat and the dog are enemies; they make war on each other.' I say that we too, in this room, are a little one and a big one and he is afraid that war might break out between us. He replies that this is possible, but he is sure I won't believe him when he tells me he has seen an *enormous cat* in the street, which he describes in detail.

(Today, I think he is shrugging off my interpretations, which he feels to be heavy and slippery; like the lining, they fail to stick. This revives his spirits and he is able to resume his play with new projects – the dog (trust, a bond) and the rabbit (a peace-loving animal). In other words, a relaxed, trustful climate replaces that of distrust, the dog and the cat being different in the sense that they are two different mental climates. Instead, I interpret the cat and the dog in the transference, as myself and himself, and this generates an enormous cat, representing enormous distrust.)

I tell him that, at times, he would like to be the enormous cat and to frighten me. He says he wants to see if he can put the dog together again because he remembers it, but wants to be sure. He adds: 'But the rabbit represents peace, and perhaps I couldn't do the head properly because I don't really know what peace is like, and we need to find out a few more things before we get there.'

Taking some plasticine, he says he wants to make some other animals; he takes the animals – for the first time – out of the toy box and separates them into two piles, one with the horse, hen, dog and crocodile, and the other with all the other species; then he puts them all aside except for the crocodile and starts copying them in white plasticine on a large scale (about 3:1) . . .

When I ask him what the crocodile suggests to him, he answers: 'War, battles, quarrels.' I suggest he might mean he is more familiar with war and quarrels, both between Daddy and Mummy and with me, and perhaps he feels there is fighting rather than peace inside himself. He nods thoughtfully, signifying agreement. The crocodile's head continues to protrude.

I say that, while warring, this crocodile actually loses its head. 'I know what you mean when you say there are quarrels and fighting between us; we can't find out new things and we go forward slowly.'

(Once again I have interpreted his wish to frighten me in the transference, instead of picking up the new wave of distrust that is forming. Massimo then tries to rebuild a climate of trust: he doesn't want to forget the original 'dog'. In my subsequent interventions, I do not succeed in helping him to find a peaceful, farm-like climate (the rabbit). My interventions make him reject other possible climates (emotional atmospheres) and banish him to the savannah, where the crocodile exemplifies a dangerous place of battles, fights and skirmishes rather than of welcoming and peaceful containment. I am stressing his α-function and ♀♂ beyond their capacity for acceptance and transformation, thus generating persecution.)

A few general comments are now in order.

Interpretation

Interpretation will be more mutative if it takes the form of a factor of growth rather than of persecution (Lussana 1984; Rosenfeld 1987; Tuckett 1989; Speziale-Bagliacca 1991, 1998; Bianchedi 1996).

I recall what happened once when I gave a premature transference interpretation: the young woman patient started up and said: 'I've been stung by some creature; look at the weal, all red and swollen.' The interpretation was an intense source of turbulence; it resulted in the formation of an α-element, an emotional pictogram that remained behind like an inner Polaroid photograph. However, we can discern its 'narrative derivative' – 'I've been stung by some creature; look at the weal, all red and swollen' – which tells of a pictogram that has conferred form, colour and expression on an experience of surprise, pain and irritation.

Other intensely communicative narrative derivatives could have been chosen – for instance, 'When I was small, my father used to slap me without warning, leaving a mark behind' or 'I saw a lorry on TV that went through a red light and crashed into a line of cars' or 'At nursery school my little brother was knocked bleeding to the ground by a bully' or 'I remember an episode of *Emergency Room* where some people were injured by robbers and had to be revived: there was so much blood' – and so on. There are in fact an infinite number of other possible narrative derivatives of the same α-element, as well as, perhaps, a graphic derivative (a drawing of an arrow hitting a bear and making it bleed), a play-type derivative (a bounding tiger that suddenly sinks its fangs into a hunter), a sensory derivative (an acute stomach ache), a motor derivative (bumping into the corner of a table and hurting oneself) or an oneiric derivative (reporting a dream in which the patient's foot is injured by a shard of glass).

In my view, interpretations must often take the form of an unsaturated, polysemic event (Guignard 1997, 1998) that opens the way to new meaning (Andrade de Azevedo 1996) and permits a narrative development to which the patient contributes constructively and actively at all times (Nissim Momigliano 1991, 1992).

As Riolo (1997) points out, there are symbolic systems with the function of deciphering meaning and others whose function is to produce it. Psychoanalysis is a system directed towards the generation of new thoughts, which, however, require a space of non-saturation in which they can oscillate, and, as Guignard would say, there is always a risk of *interprétations-bouchon* blocking the development of thought.

That said, it is of course sometimes necessary to 'close off the sense' with saturated transference interventions (Spillius 1983, 1988; Rocha Barros 1996).

Signals emitted by the text

Patients give constant signals of their experience of our interpretative interventions (Muñoz 1998). What the patient says can be seen as generated by the repetition of his history (which, in part, it is), or as a projection on to the outside world of fantasies from his internal world (and this too, in part, is the case) – but it can also be considered as issuing from the immediacy of the here and now, as a real-time response to the emotional afferences of the relational instant. This last approach enables us constantly to modulate our interventions in such a way as to permit an expansion of thinkability.

The characters of the session

As stated in Chapter 7, these will be seen in very different ways according to one's chosen model. For instance, when Massimo mentions his 'cat', the 'dog' or the 'rabbit', these characters can be thought of mainly on the realistic level: the acquisition of the cat and the promise of the dog are certainly significant events in the real external life of Massimo, enabling him to undertake deeper affective cathexes and to emerge from his defensive shell. However, the cat and dog can also be attributed to intrapsychic forms of functioning, to Massimo's internal objects, and will in this case be interpreted as such. In yet another model, they are viewed as signals of relational qualities of the couple at that particular instant:

trust, suspicion, closeness and fear succeed each other in the consulting room, and what matters is how they are *transformed* in the present.

Some time ago, Marcella, a 15-year-old patient who came twice a week, told me that at school there were only two toilets for 15 girls and that it wasn't easy to use them because they had to pass some boys on the way. I said only: 'Two toilets for 15 girls is really not very much; it isn't easy to show that you have needs in front of other people; that problem certainly has to be solved.' Marcella smiled and drew a little dog – which, I thought, was something born of the session on account of my unsaturated intervention. (Had I chosen a different model, I might have thought she was telling me about a real external problem, or I could have given a saturated interpretation to the effect that she wanted to have more than two sessions.)

A few days later, Marcella was talking about school and the toilets again; it was one of the last sessions of the day and I was tired, so that I failed to notice her signal of my deficient availability (not enough toilets), and told her: 'I think you are telling me that two sessions a week is not very much and that it isn't easy for you to show me that you have needs.' Marcella looked at me sadly and said: 'I was looking out of the window at school and saw a man with a moustache hitting a puppy with a big stick: he hurt it so badly that he eventually killed it.' My saturated interpretation was experienced as something very violent that inflicted wounds, and that not only failed to cause anything to be born, but also killed off something – trust – that was coming into being.

So we must always pay close attention to the response to our interpretations, admittedly regarding it as something that draws on the patient's history and internal world, but bearing in mind that it also has to do with the here and now of our relationship with the patient. The analyst can constantly and constructively modify the field by monitoring it and varying his own interpretative setting.

Of course, what applies to a verbal response is also true of its 'play' counterpart: if Marcella had been 7 years old, she might well have expressed the same material in play instead of in words.

Play

In view of the foregoing, it is readily understandable that I found the title of a recent symposium – 'Play as a mediator between the internal and external worlds' – particularly felicitous in that it casts play as the central intermediary between the world of fantasy (that is, in my Bionian dialect, α-elements) and the external world (in my dialect, relationships with others). Play is the ludic derivative, or carrier, that makes α-elements communicable.

I am convinced of the unity of mental functioning – i.e. that what applies to children also applies to adolescents or adults (Ferro 1992) – and also that play, drawing, acting out and narration all have the same function of mediating what is happening in the depths of mental life and of making it knowable.

I further believe that the kind of 'play' concretely enshrined in the use of characters, objects or animals can be unconditionally equated with the more abstract narrations of an adult patient, so that instead of a game with a she-tiger we have, say, an account of supper with the patient's mother-in-law.

What matters is the form of the analyst's participation in the play: whether play in the literal sense or verbal play, it must be able to develop freely without premature closure of its meaning.

Notes

1 Narrations and interpretations

1 According to Bion (1963), to be effective an interpretation must extend into the field of 'sense, myth and passion'.
2 Translator's note: to avoid clumsy constructions, where applicable the masculine personal pronoun and possessive adjective are used throughout for both sexes.
3 The inclusion of narrative transformation among the various types of transformations is due to Corrao (1991).
4 –K stands for the opposite of authentic knowledge. Column 2 of Bion's Grid is the column of lies (including interpretative lies) aimed at avoiding the anxiety generated by truth.
5 The reference is to Bernard L. Kowalski's 1969 film *Krakatoa, East of Java*, inspired by the catastrophic eruption of the Krakatoa volcano that submerged many Indonesian islands in 1883.
6 The reference is to Steven Spielberg's 1993 film *Jurassic Park*, in which the disabling of the security system of a theme park containing dinosaurs bred from DNA fragments causes these animals to embark on an orgy of devouring and destruction.
7 Translator's note: Fausto Coppi was an Italian champion cyclist who died in 1960.
8 Translator's note: Alda Merini is an Italian poet, born 1931.
9 Translator's note: the name Quantestorie means 'Manystories'.
10 Translator's note: the Italian word *lettino* can mean either bed or couch.

2 Telling ourselves stories with, perhaps, a grain of truth

1 This ten-minute interval between patients is in my view of fundamental importance, acting as it does as a kind of decompression chamber that enables one to exit one story and prepare to enter another, with a minimum of contamination.
2 Riolo (1989) stresses that a thought arising in the session from one mind only is somehow a mendacious thought (–K).
3 Translator's note: the Italian word for railwayman is *ferroviere*, which contains the analyst's surname *Ferro*.

4 Translator's note: *L'Unità* is the Italian Communist newspaper; the title means 'Unity'.
5 Translator's note: Serenase is the Italian commercial name for haloperidol.
6 Translator's note: 'tranquil' is *sereno* in Italian – a play on the name of the tranquillizer Serenase.
7 Translator's note: Tinto Brass is an Italian erotic filmmaker.
8 Translator's note: the Italian word *griglia* means both grill and grid (i.e. Bion's Grid), while the Italian for iron is *ferro*, which is also the analyst's surname; 'F' is the initial letter of the Italian word for iron and of the analyst's name, but the reference is also to Row F of Bion's Grid.
9 Translator's note: the Italian word for uncovering can also mean discovering.

3 In praise of Row C: psychoanalysis as a particular form of literature

1 Translator's note: both *Qui* and *Qua* mean 'here'; *Quo* does not mean anything. The explanation follows.
2 Translator's note: the Italian phrase can mean either 'threw a pen' or 'plucked a feather'.
3 Translator's note: the Italian word *fumare* (to smoke) also means 'to fume'.

4 Sexuality as a narrative genre or dialect in the analyst's consulting room: a radical vertex

1 I shall not consider sexual acting out in the analytic session because, while on the one hand (on the analyst's side) it is a matter of the analyst's own pathology, on the other (with regard to the patient) it has to do with the many different forms of acting in.
2 'W' here refers to a 'whole response' of the field itself with emotional coloration, by analogy with Rorschach's W.
3 Translator's note: the reference is to Pedro Almodóvar's 1990 film *Átame* ('Tie me up'). In Italian, if the stress is on the first syllable (*Légami*), the meaning would be 'tie me up', but if it is on the second syllable (*Legámi*), the word would mean 'bonds'.
4 Stephen Frears' 1996 film *Mary Reilly*.
5 The Italian word *ferro* (which is also the analyst's name) means 'iron', an English word that to Italian ears suggests *ira* (ire, or incontinent rage).
6 *Memory* is a children's game using cards of which each pair has a different picture on one side, while all the cards have the same pattern on the other. An α-element is in reality a much more complex and interlinked emotional pictogram, but for the sake of clarity I have imagined it grossly oversimplified, as if it contained a single elementary image; a better analogy might be with a tarot card.
7 A balpha-element is a useful concept which denotes a partially digested β-element that can be stored precisely as an 'undigested fact', but differs both from α-elements and from unprocessed β-elements. The analogy is with incomplete ruminative predigestion.

8 The fabula is the basic schema of the narration, the syntax of the characters, whereas the plot is the story as actually told, as it appears on the surface (Eco 1979).
9 Although I have discussed α-elements in purely visual terms, they are in reality more complicated, as they may also be auditory or coenaesthetic. However, the basic argument is the same.

5 The waking dream: theoretical and clinical aspects

1 Translator's note: the Italian word *sollievo* means 'relief'.
2 Translator's note: a play on words because *ferri* here means knitting needles, but is also the plural of *ferro*, which is the analyst's name.
3 Elvira Banotti is a well-known Italian feminist historian.

6 Delusion and hallucination

1 Translator's note: the reference is to Francis Bacon's 1953 painting *Study After Velázquez's Portrait of Pope Innocent X.*
2 Translator's note: Val Padana is the area around Milan and Pavia, where the analyst practises.
3 Translator's note: Piero Chiara was a Sicilian author (1913–86) who moved north.
4 There is in my view a gradient of delusional forms extending from 'waking dream flashes' to 'transformations into hallucinosis' or 'hallucinations' according to the extent to which the evacuations of α-, balpha- or β-elements are internal. However, whereas the visual phenomena are indicative of the immediacy of the disturbance of the α-function or of ♀♂, delusional narrations involve in addition a pathology of the signification and resignification of the world and of the world of the emotions. I recall the first delusional patient I treated as a psychiatrist: an elderly woman, she had lost her only daughter as a little girl while she herself was still young; having been unable to work through her mourning, more than twenty years later she was still caring for a rag doll, which she would not let out of her sight and which she said was her daughter. The evacuation of balpha-elements into the doll in effect brought it to life, or protected the patient from catastrophic collapse.
5 Translator's note: Giorgio Scerbanenco was an Italian thriller writer (1911–69), born in Kiev.
6 Translator's note: Demetrio Pianelli is a character created by Emilio De Marchi (1851–1901), who depicted the Milanese urban middle classes.
7 Translator's note: the Castle of Fénis is in the Val d'Aosta.
8 Translator's note: cappuccino coffee is so called, according to the Concise Oxford Dictionary, because its colour resembles that of a Capuchin's habit.
9 Translator's note: this is a reference to the Italian system of driving licences – class A for motorcycles, B for cars, C for lorries and E for public service vehicles. The patient invents a non-existent class G, the initial letter of the Italian word *guarigione*, which means cure.
10 This is a phrase in our private analytic language meaning 'to lose control'.

11 This concerns an analytic function of mine, because I had certainly not yet understood that the anxiety was due to a gap that needed to be bridged.
12 Translator's note: the Italian word is *palazzo*, which means a large building such as an office block. However, in this context it also has the connotation of the analyst's consulting room, where the analytic work is done, but may also imply confusion of ideas, or alternatively 'coming straight to the point'.

7 Characters in literature and in the analyst's consulting room

1 See note 8 in Chapter 4.
2 From Greimas on, an anti-anthropomorphic approach has prevailed, in which a character is not necessarily a human agent, but may be any element assigned figurative status at surface level that takes the form of a profound syntactic unit (an actant). A character can thus be an animal, a house or a concept. As Lotman (1970) notes, once the anthropomorphizing discriminant is eliminated, the character does usually prove to refer to human agents, but this is no longer necessarily so.
3 For Greimas (1966), actors are simply the various characters, whereas actants are classes of actors with similar groups of functions and spheres of action.
4 Hologram: holography is an optical technique that uses coherent light sources allowing the three-dimensional photographic reproduction of an object on a single substrate and its subsequent three-dimensional reconstruction. The most promising application is likely to be three-dimensional holographic cinematography, which would produce a *complete illusion* of the scene represented, with all the effects of the actual presence of objects (Denisyuk 1979, translated).
5 The word *Sedocalcio* can be broken down into its elements *se-do-calcio*, which means, in Italian, 'if I kick', thus expressing rage and aggression.
6 'Pesto' not only is a condiment used in Ligurian cuisine but also suggests the Italian verb *pestare*, meaning to thrash.
7 Translator's note: *ferro* means iron, but is also the analyst's name.

8 Notes on acting out, the countertransference and the transgenerational field

1 The lithograph is reproduced in Ferro (1996a: 39).
2 The narrating function: that is, the co-narrating function of analyst and patient.

9 Child and adolescent analysis: similarities and differences that mask an underlying unity

1 See note 8 in Chapter 4.

10 Play: characters, narrations and interpretations

1 Translator's note: the Italian word is *ferro*, which is also the analyst's name.

References

Aalberg, V. (1997) 'Il lavoro psicoanalitico con gli adolescenti: illustrazione di un caso clinico', *Richard e Piggle*, 5: 73–4.

Abraham, K. (1920) 'The narcissistic evaluation of excretory processes in dreams and neurosis', in *Selected Papers on Psycho-Analysis*, London: Hogarth, 1949.

—— (1922) 'The spider as a dream symbol', in *Selected Papers on Psycho-Analysis*, London: Hogarth, 1949.

Amati Mehler, J., Argentieri, S., and Canestri, J. (1990) *The Babel of the Unconscious: Mother Tongue and Foreign Languages in the Psychoanalytic Dimension*, trans. J. Whitelaw-Cucco, Madison, CT: International Universities Press, 1993.

Andersen, H.C. (1847) 'The shadow', in *The Stories of Hans Christian Andersen*, trans. D. Crone Frank and J. Frank, London: Granta, 2004.

Anderson, R. (1993) 'Some observations on the value of child analysis within the psychoanalytic world', *Psychoanalysis in Europe*, 41: 64–8.

—— (1997) 'Esigenze della formazione al lavoro psicoanalitico con gli adolescenti', *Richard e Piggle*, 5: 63–6.

Andrade de Azevedo, A.M. (1996) 'Interpretation: revelation or creation?', paper discussed at the symposium *Bion in São Paulo: Resonances*, São Paulo, 14 November.

Arlow, J. (1985) 'The structural hypothesis', in A. Rothstein (ed.) *Models of the Mind: Their Relationships to Clinical Work*, New York: International Universities Press.

Arrigoni, M.R., and Barbieri, G.L. (1998) *Narrazione e psicoanalisi*, Milan: Raffaello Cortina.

Barale, F., and Ferro, A. (1992). 'Negative therapeutic reactions and microfractures in analytic communication', in L. Nissim Momigliano and A. Robutti (eds) *Shared Experience: The Psychoanalytic Dialogue*, London: Karnac.

—— (1993) 'Sufrimiento mental en el analista y sueños de contratransferencia', *Revista de Psicoanálisis de Madrid*, 17: 56–72.

Barale, F., and Ucelli, S. (1992) 'Il racconto della storia e lo strato roccioso della memoria', *Gli Argonauti*, 52: 35–45.

Baranger, M. (1959) 'Mala fe, identidad y omnipotencia', in W. Baranger and M. Baranger, *Problemas del campo psicoanalítico*, Buenos Aires: Kargieman.

—— (1992) 'La mente del analista: de la escucha a la interpretación', *Revista de Psicoanálisis*, 49: 223.

Baranger, M., and Baranger, W. (1961–2) 'La situación analítica como campo dinámico', *Revista Uruguaya de Psicoanálisis*, 4: 3–54.

—— (1964) 'Insight in the analytic situation', in R.E. Litman (ed.) *Psychoanalysis in the Americas*, New York: International Universities Press, 1966.

—— (1969) *Problemas del campo psicoanalítico*, Buenos Aires: Kargieman.

Baranger, M., Baranger, W., and Mom, J. (1983) 'Process and non-process in analytic work', *International Journal of Psychoanalysis*, 64: 1–15.

—— (1988) 'The infantile psychic trauma from us to Freud: pure trauma, retroactivity and reconstruction', *International Journal of Psychoanalysis*, 69: 113–28.

Baranger, W. (1960) 'El sueño como medio analítico de comunicación', in W. Baranger and M. Baranger, *Problemas del campo psicoanalítico*, Buenos Aires: Kargieman.

Baranger, W., Zac de Goldstein, R., and Goldstein, N. (1994) *Artesanías psicoanalíticas*, Buenos Aires: Kargieman.

Barthes, R. (1964) *Elements of Semiology*, trans. A. Lavers and C. Smith, London: Cape, 1967.

Berberich, E. (1990) 'On the way to interpretation in the transference, and the consequences', *Psychoanalysis in Europe*, 34: 35–44.

—— (1993) 'Some comments on the crisis around frequency', *Psychoanalysis in Europe*, 41: 69–71.

Bernstein, I. (1975) 'On the technique of child and adolescent analysis', *Journal of the American Psychoanalytic Association*, 23: 190–232.

Bezoari, M., and Ferro, A. (1989) 'Ascolto, interpretazioni e funzioni trasformative nel dialogo analitico', *Rivista di Psicoanalisi*, 35: 1015–51.

—— (1990a) 'Elementos de un modelo del campo analítico: los agregados funcionales', *Revista de Psicoanálisis*, 5/6: 847–61.

—— (1990b) 'Parole, immagini, affetti: l'avventura del senso nell'incontro analitico', in G. Bartoli (ed.) *In due dietro il lettino. Scritti in onore di Luciana Nissim Momigliano*, Castrovillari: Teda Edizioni.

—— (1991a) 'A oscilação dos significados afetos no trabalho da parelha analítica', *Revista Brasileira de Psicanálise*, 26: 365–74.

—— (1991b) 'From a play between "parts" to transformations in the couple: psychoanalysis in a bipersonal field', in L. Nissim Momigliano and A. Robutti (eds) *Shared Experience: The Psychoanalytic Dialogue*, London: Karnac, 1992.

—— (1992a) 'El sueño dentro de una teoría del campo: los agregados funcionales', *Revista de Psicoanálisis*, 49: 957–77.

—— (1992b) 'I personaggi della seduta come aggregati funzionali del campo analitico', *Notiziario SPI*, Supplemento 2, pp. 103–15, Rome: Borla.

—— (1994a) 'Listening, interpreting and psychic change in the analytic dialogue', *International Forum of Psychoanalysis*, 3: 35–41.

—— (1994b) 'Il posto del sogno all'interno di una teoria del campo analitico', *Rivista di Psicoanalisi*, 40: 251–72.

Bianchedi, E.T. (1995) 'Creative writers and dream-work-alpha', in *On Freud's Creative Writers and Day-Dreaming*, London: Yale University Press.

—— (1996) 'Interpretación: ¿Relación o creación? y/o ¿Evolución / intersección / decisión / construcción?', paper discussed at the symposium *Bion in São Paulo: Resonances*, São Paulo, 14 November.

Bion, W.R. (1962) *Learning from Experience*, London: Heinemann.
—— (1963) *Elements of Psycho-Analysis*, London: Heinemann.
—— (1965) *Transformations*, London: Heinemann.
—— (1966) 'Catastrophic change', *Bulletin of the British Psycho-Analytical Society*, no. 5.
—— (1970) *Attention and Interpretation*, London: Tavistock.
—— (1975) *A Memoir of the Future, Book 1, The Dream*, Rio de Janeiro: Imago.
—— (1978) *Four Discussions with W.R. Bion*, Strath Tay, Perthshire: Clunie Press.
—— (1980) *Bion in New York and São Paulo*, Strath Tay, Perthshire: Clunie Press.
—— (1985) *The Italian Seminars*, London: Karnac, 2005.
—— (ed.) (1987) *Clinical Seminars and Four Papers*, Abingdon: Fleetwood.
—— (ed.) (1992) *Cogitations*, London: Karnac.
—— (ed.) (1997) *Taming Wild Thoughts*, London: Karnac.
Bion Talamo, P. (1987) 'Perché non possiamo dirci bioniani', *Gruppo e funzione analitica*, 8: 279–284.
Bleger, J. (1966) *Psicohigiene y psicología institucional*, Buenos Aires: Paidós.
Bolognini, S. (1997) 'Empatia e patologie gravi', in A. Correali and R. Rinaldi, *Quale psicoanalisi per le psicosi?*, Milan: Raffaello Cortina.
Bonaminio, V. (1993) 'Del non interpretare', *Rivista di Psicoanalisi*, 39: 453–77.
Borges, J.L. (1941a) 'The garden of forking paths', trans. H. Temple and R. Todd, in *Ficciones*, London: Everyman, 1993.
—— (1941b) 'The library of Babel', trans. A. Kerrigan, in *Ficciones*, London: Everyman, 1993.
Borgogno, F. (1997) 'Parla il campo: immagini e pensieri', in E. Gaburri (ed.) *Emozione e interpretazione*, Turin: Bollati Boringhieri.
Brenman, E. (1977) 'The narcissism of the analyst: its effects in clinical practice', *Psychoanalysis in Europe*, 13: 20–7.
Brenman, E. and Pick, I. (1985) 'Working-through in the counter-transference', *International Journal of Psychoanalysis*, 66: 157–66.
Britton, R. (1989) 'The missing link: parental sexuality in the Oedipus complex', in J. Steiner (ed.) *The Oedipus Complex Today*, London: Karnac.
Cahn, R. (1997) 'Specificità della formazione al lavoro psicoanalitico con gli adolescenti', *Richard e Piggle*, 5: 57–62.
Calvino, I. (1964) 'Preface', in *The Path to the Nest of Spiders*, trans. A. Colquhoun, New York: Ecco Press, 1976.
—— (1979) *If on a Winter's Night a Traveler*, trans. W. Weaver, New York: Harcourt Brace Jovanovich, 1981.
—— (1980) *Una pietra sopra: Discorsi di letteratura e società*, Turin: Einaudi.
—— (1988) *Six Memos for the Next Millennium*, New York: Vintage, 1993.
Carels, N. (1998) 'The double – reflection and agent of psychic transformations', *Psychoanalysis in Europe*, 50: 5–17.
Catz de Katz, H. (1996) 'Some reflections on the analyst's daydreaming: the analytic field and its possible transformations', conference draft paper, Bion 1997, Turin. Online. Available http://www.sicap.it/~merciai/bion/papers/catz.htm (accessed 10 May 2005).
Cavazzoni, E. (1987) *The Voice of the Moon*, trans. E. Emery, London: Serpent's Tail, 1990.

Collini, S. (1995) 'Interpretation terminable and interminable', introduction to U. Eco, R. Rorty, J. Culler and C. Brooke-Rose, *Interpretation and Overinterpretation*, S. Collini (ed.), Cambridge: Cambridge University Press.

Corrao, F. (1986) 'Il concetto di campo come modello teorico', in *Orme*, vol. 2, Milan: Raffaello Cortina, 1998.

—— (1987) 'Il narrativo come categoria psicoanalitica', in *Orme*, vol. 1, Milan: Raffaello Cortina, 1998.

—— (1991) 'Trasformazioni narrative', in *Orme*, vol. 1, Milan: Raffaello Cortina, 1998.

—— (1992) *Modelli psicoanalitici: mito, passione, memoria*, Rome: Laterza.

Culler, J. (1982) *On Deconstruction*, Ithaca, NY: Cornell University Press.

Decobert, S., and Sacco, F. (eds) (1995) *Le Dessin dans le travail psychanalytique avec l'enfant*, Ramonville-Saint-Agne: Erès.

De León de Bernardi, B. (1988) 'Interpretación, acercamiento analítico y creatividad', *Revista Uruguaya de Psicoanálisis*, 68: 57–68.

—— (1991) 'Las teorías del analista y los cambios en la consideración de la dinámica del proceso psicoanalítico', *Revista de Psicoanálisis*, 47: 49–58.

De Levita, D.J. (1993) 'A few notes on frequency', *Psychoanalysis in Europe*, 41: 97–102.

De Man, P. (1971) *Blindness and Insight: Essays in the Rhetoric of Contemporary Criticism*, New York: Oxford University Press.

—— (1986) *The Resistance to Theory*, Minneapolis, MN: University of Minnesota Press.

Denisyuk, Yu.N. (1979) 'Olografia', in *Enciclopedia Europea*, Milan: Garzanti.

Derrida, J. (1977) *Limited Inc.: abc . . .*, Baltimore, MD: Johns Hopkins University Press.

De Simone, G., and Fornari, B. (1988) 'Melanie Klein e la scuola inglese', in A.A. Semi (ed.) *Trattato di Psicoanalisi*, vol. 1, Milan: Raffaello Cortina Editore.

Di Chiara, G. (1979) 'Il predicato analitico del paziente', *Rivista di Psicoanalisi*, 25: 131–3.

—— (1992) 'Meeting, telling and parting: three basic factors in the psychoanalytic experience', in L. Nissim Momigliano and A. Robutti (eds) *Shared Experience: The Psychoanalytic Dialogue*, London: Karnac.

Diderot, D. (1796) *Jacques the Fatalist and his Master*, trans. J.R. Loy, New York: Collier, 1962.

Dostoevsky, F. (1846) *The Double*, Mineola, NY: Dover, 1997.

Eco, U. (1962) *The Open Work*, Cambridge, MA: Harvard University Press, 1989.

—— (1979) *The Role of the Reader*, Bloomington, IN: Indiana University Press, 1981.

—— (1990) *The Limits of Interpretation*, Bloomington, IN: Indiana University Press.

Ecu, U., Rorty, R., Culler, J., and Brooke-Rose, C. (1992) *Interpretation and Overinterpretation*, S. Collini (ed.), Cambridge: Cambridge University Press.

Eizirik, C.L. (1993) 'Entre a escuta e a interpretação: um estudio da neutralidade psicanalítica', *Revista de Psicanálise da SPPA*, 1: 19–42.

—— (1996) 'Panel report: psychic reality and clinical technique', *International Journal of Psychoanalysis*, 77: 37–41.

—— (1998) 'Masculinidade e feminilidade na virada do milênio: uma breve reflexão psicanalítica', *Revista de Psicanálise da Sociedade Psicanalítica de Porto Alegre*, 5: 165–71.

Eskelinen de Folch, T. (1988) 'Communication and containing in child analysis: towards terminability', *International Journal of Psychoanalysis*, 69: 105–12.

Etchegoyen, R.H. (1986) *The Fundamentals of Psychoanalytic Technique*, trans. P. Pitchon, London: Karnac, 1991.

—— (1996) 'Some views on psychic reality', *International Journal of Psychoanalysis*, 77: 1–14.

Eva, A.C. (1995) 'Sexualidade em psicanálise', *Forum de Psicanálise*, São Paulo: Sociedade Psicanalítica de São Paulo.

Faimberg, H. (1988) 'A l'écoute du télescopage des générations: pertinence psychanalytique du concept', *Topique*, 42: 223–8.

—— (1989) 'Sans mémoire et sans désir: à qui s'adressait Bion', *Revue Française de Psychanalyse*, 53: 1453–61.

—— (1992) 'The countertransference position and the countertransference', *International Journal of Psychoanalysis*, 73: 541–6.

Faria, C.G. (1998) 'Sexualidade e estrutura psíquica', *Revista de Psicanálise de Porto Alegre*, 5: 239–46.

Ferro, A. (1987) 'Il mondo alla rovescia: l'inversione del flusso delle identificazioni proiettive', *Rivista di Psicoanalisi*, 33: 59–77.

—— (1991a) 'La mente del analista en su trabajo: problemas, riesgos, necesidades', *Revista de Psicoanálisis*, 5/6: 1159–77.

—— (1991b) 'From Raging Bull to Theseus: the long path of a transformation', *International Journal of Psychoanalysis*, 72: 417–25.

—— (1992) *The Bi-Personal Field: Experiences in Child Analysis*, London: Routledge, 1999.

—— (1993a) 'Il disegno e le parole come "disegno" all'interno di una teoria del campo', *Richard e Piggle*, 1: 18.

—— (1993b) 'Mundos posibles y capacidades negativas del analista en su trabajo', *Anuario Ibérico de Psicoanálisis*, 3: 14.

—— (1993c) 'The impasse within a theory of the analytic field: possible vertices of observation', *International Journal of Psychoanalysis*, 74: 917–29.

—— (1993d) 'Zwei Autoren auf der Suche nach Personen: Die Beziehung, das Feld, die Geschichte', *Psyche*, 47: 951–72.

—— (1993e) 'From hallucination to dream: from evacuation to the tolerability of pain in the analysis of a preadolescent', *Psychoanalytic Review*, 80: 389–404.

—— (1994a) 'Del campo e dei suoi eventi', *Quaderni di Psicoterapia Infantile*, 30: 39–52.

—— (1994b) 'Gruppalità interne di relazione e di campo nell'analisi duale', *Gruppo e Funzione Analitica*, Quaderni, 1, Rome: Borla.

—— (1994c) 'El diálogo analítico: mundos posibles y transformaciones en el campo analítico', *Revista de Psicoanálisis*, 51: 771–90.

—— (1994d) 'Criterios sobre la analizabilidad y el final del análisis dentro de una teoría del campo', *Revista de Psicoanálisis*, 51: 97–114.

—— (1995a) 'Il narratore e la paura', in M. Noziglia (ed.) *Giocare e pensare*, Milan: Guerini e Associati.

—— (1995b) 'Ricordare, ripetere, trasformare', paper presented at the APA Congress, Buenos Aires, October.

—— (1995c) 'Giocare e pensare', in M. Noziglia (ed.) *Giocare e pensare*, Milan: Guerini e Associati.

—— (1995d) 'L'oscillazione tra capacità negativa e fatto prescelto nel campo analitico', paper presented at the APA Conference, Buenos Aires, October.

—— (1995e) 'Lo sviluppo del concetto di campo in Europa', paper presented at a meeting in honour of W. Baranger, Buenos Aires, October.

—— (1996a) *In the Analyst's Consulting Room*, trans. P. Slotkin, Hove: Brunner-Routledge, 2002.
—— (1996b) 'Los personajes del cuarto de análisis: ¿Qué realidad?', *Revista de Psicoanálisis de Madrid*, 23: 133–42.
—— (1996c) 'Sexualidade como gênero narrativo', paper discussed at the symposium *Bion in São Paulo: Resonances*, São Paulo, 14 November.
—— (1996d) 'Carla's panic attacks: insight and transformations: what comes out of the cracks: monster or nascent thoughts?', *International Journal of Psychoanalysis*, 77: 997–1011.
—— (1996e) 'Elógio da fileira C: a psicanálise como forma particular de literatura', in L.C. Uchoa Junqueira Filho (ed.) *Silêncios e luzes: sobre a experiência psíquica do vazio e da forma*, São Paulo: Casa do Psicólogo, 1998.
—— (1996f) 'Entrevista com Antonino Ferro', *IDE* (São Paulo), 29.
—— (1997a) 'Giocare per poter pensare', in D. Canciani and P. Sartori (eds) *Dire, fare, giocare*, Rome: Armando.
—— (1997b) 'La mente dell'analista tra capacità negative e fatto prescelto: la costruzione di storie', in G. Rugi and E. Gaburri (eds) *Il campo gruppale*, Rome: Borla.
—— (1997c) 'La sessualità come genere narrativo o dialetto nella stanza d'analisi: un vertice radicale', in P. Bion, F. Borgogno and S. Merciai (eds) *Lavorare con Bion*, Rome: Borla, 1998.
—— (1998a) 'Unity of analysis underlying the similarities and differences in the analysis of children and adolescents', *Psychoanalysis in Europe*, 50: 48–58.
—— (1998b) 'Le jeu: personnages, récits, interprétations', paper presented at the Fourth EPF Conference on Child and Adolescent Analysis, Stockholm, 25–6 April, and the SEPEA Conference, Paris, 26 September.
—— (1998c) 'Il sogno della veglia: teoria e clinica', *Rivista di Psicoanalisi*, 44: 117–28.
—— (1998d) 'Antonino Ferro em São Paulo', in M.O. de A. França and M. Petricciani (eds) *Seminários*, São Paulo: Editora Sociedade Brasileira de Psicanálise de São Paulo, Acervo Psicanalítico.
—— (1998e) 'Continente inadequado e violência das emoções: dinossauros e tartarugas', lecture to the São Paulo and Porto Alegre Psychoanalytic Centre, November.
Ferro, A. and Meregnani, A. (1998) 'The inversion of the flow of projective identification in the analyst at work', *Australian Journal of Psychotherapy*, 16: 94–112.
Ferruta, A. (1998) 'Tra Corinto e Tebe. Il controtransfert all'incrocio tra riconoscimento e accecamento', *Rivista di Psicoanalisi*, 44: 295–308.
Fonagy, P. and Sandler, A.-M. (1995) 'On transference and its interpretation', *Bulletin of the European Psychoanalytical Federation*, 45: 5–26.
França, M.O.A.F. (1996) 'To act, to hallucinate, to dream', paper discussed at the symposium *Bion in São Paulo: Resonances*, São Paulo, November.
Freud, S. (1900) *The Interpretation of Dreams*, in *Standard Edition*, vols 4–5, London: Hogarth.
—— (1905) *Three Essays on the Theory of Sexuality*, in *Standard Edition*, vol. 7, London: Hogarth.
—— (1909) 'Notes upon a case of obsessional neurois', in *Standard Edition*, vol. 10, London: Hogarth.
—— (1913) 'The occurrence in dreams of material from fairy-tales', in *Standard Edition*, vol. 12, London: Hogarth.

—— (1914) 'From the history of an infantile neurosis ("Wolf Man")', in *Standard Edition*, vol. 17, London: Hogarth.
—— (1924) 'A note upon the "mystic writing-pad"', in *Standard Edition*, vol. 19, London: Hogarth.
—— (1937) 'Constructions in analysis', in *Standard Edition*, vol. 23, London: Hogarth.
Gaburri, E. (ed.) (1997) *Emozione e interpretazione*, Turin: Bollati Boringhieri.
Gaburri, E. and Ferro, A. (1988) 'Gli sviluppi kleiniani e Bion', in A. Semi (ed.) *Trattato di psicoanalisi*, vol. 1, Milan: Raffaello Cortina.
Gadda, C.E. (1958) *I viaggi e la morte*, Milan: Garzanti.
—— (1982) *Il tempo e le opere*, Milan: Adelphi.
—— (1992) *Saggi, giornali, favole e altri scritti*, Milan: Garzanti.
Gibeault, A. (1991) 'Interpretation and transference', *Psychoanalysis in Europe*, 36: 47–61.
Goijman, L., and Kancyper, L. (eds) (1998) *Clínica psicoanalítica de niños y adolescentes*, Buenos Aires: Lumen.
Goldmann, L. (1964) *Pour une sociologie du roman*, Paris: Gallimard.
Green, A. (1973) *The Fabric of Affect in the Psychoanalytic Discourse*, trans. A. Sheridan, London: Routledge, 1999.
—— (1995) 'Has sexuality anything to do with psychoanalysis?', *International Journal of Psychoanalysis*, 76: 871–83.
Greimas, A.J. (1966) *Structural Semantics*, trans. H.S. Gill, New Delhi: Bahri.
—— (1970) *On Meaning: Selected Writings in Semiotic Theory*, trans. P.J. Perron and F.H. Collins, London: F. Pinter, 1987.
Guignard, F. (1987) 'The setting and countertransference in child analysis', *Psychoanalysis in Europe*, 29: 39–52.
—— (1996) *Au vif de l'infantile*, Lausanne: Delachaux et Niestlé.
—— (1997) *Epître à l'objet*, Paris: Presses Universitaires de France.
—— (1998) 'The interpretation of oedipal configurations in child analysis', *Psychoanalysis in Europe*, 50: 33–41.
Hamon, P. (1972) 'Pour un statut sémiologique du personnage', in R. Barthes, W. Kayser, W.C. Booth and P. Hamon, *Poétique du récit*, Paris: Seuil, 1977.
Heimann, P. (1955) 'A combination of defence mechanisms in paranoid states', in M. Klein, P. Heimann and R. Money-Kyrle (eds) *New Directions in Psycho-Analysis: The Significance of Infant Conflict in the Pattern of Adult Behaviour*, London: Tavistock.
Hesse, H. (1927) *Steppenwolf*, trans. B. Creighton, London: Secker, 1929.
Jakobson, R. (1963) *Essais de linguistique générale*, Paris: Minuit.
Joyce, J. (1937) *Ulysses*, London: Penguin, 2000.
—— (1939) *Finnegans Wake*, London: Faber.
Kaës, R., Faimberg, H., Enriquez, M., and Baranes, J.J. (1993) *Transmission de la vie psychique entre générations*, Paris: Dunod.
Kancyper, L. (1997) *La confrontación generacional*, Buenos Aires: Paidós.
Kernberg, O. (1993) 'Convergences and divergences in contemporary psychoanalytic technique', *International Journal of Psychoanalysis*, 74: 659–73.
—— (1996) 'Interpretação: revelação o criação?', paper discussed at the symposium *Bion in São Paulo: Resonances*, São Paulo, November.
Klein, M. (1929) 'Personification in the play of children', in *Contributions to Psycho-Analysis 1921–1945*, London: Hogarth, 1945.

—— (1961) *Narrative of a Child Analysis*, London: Hogarth, 1961.
Ladame, F. (1980) 'L'adolescent en psychanalyse: résistances intérieures et résistances extérieures', *Revue Française de Psychanalyse*, 44: 571–9.
—— (1992) 'Courtes remarques sur l'analyse des adolescents', *Revue Française de Psychanalyse*, 56: 827–35.
Laufer, M. (1997) 'Alcuni prerequisiti al lavoro psicoanalitico con gli adolescenti', *Richard e Piggle*, 5: 67–72.
—— (1998) 'The body in the psychopathology and psychoanalytic treatment of the child and the adolescent: theoretical and technical implications', *Psychoanalysis in Europe*, 50: 41–7.
Lotman, Yu.M. (1970) *The Structure of the Artistic Text*, trans. R. Vroon, Ann Arbor, MI: University of Michigan, 1977.
Lukács, G. (1946) *Balzac, Stendhal, Zola*, Budapest: Hungária.
—— (1948) *Karl Marx und Friedrich Engels als Literaturhistoriker*, Berlin: Aufbau-Verlag.
—— (1955) *The Historical Novel*, trans. H. Mitchell and S. Mitchell, Lincoln, NE: University of Nebraska Press, 1962.
Lussana, P. (1984) 'Evoluzione della qualità funzioni del contenitore-seno nell'analisi di un tredicenne e nella Madonna con bambino di Caravaggio', in *L'adolescente, lo psicoanalista, l'artista, una visione binoculare dell'adolescenza*, Rome: Borla, 1992.
Luzés, P. (1995) 'Edipo nella Cattedrale', Seminar at the Centro milanese di psicoanalisi, June.
McDougall, J. (1995) *The Many Faces of Eros: A Psychoanalytic Exploration of Human Sexuality*, New York: Norton.
Mächtlinger, V. (1987) 'On being an analyst of children and adults', *Psychoanalysis in Europe*, 29: 53–65.
Mancia, M. (1994a) *From Oedipus to Dream*, London: Karnac, 1996.
—— (1994b) 'Il sogno e la sua plasticità nelle trasformazioni del campo analitico', paper presented at the Tenth National Congress of the SPI, Rimini, October.
—— (1995) *Percorsi*, Turin: Bollati Boringhieri.
Manfredi Turillazzi, S. (1978) 'Interpretazione dell'agire e interpretazione come agire', *Rivista di Psicoanalisi*, 24: 223–40.
Marcus, I.M. (1980) 'Countertransference and the psychoanalytic process in children and adolescents', *Psychoanalytic Study of the Child*, 35: 285–98.
Markman, H. (1997) 'Play in the treatment of adolescents', *Psychoanalytic Quarterly*, 66: 190–218.
Marrone, G. (1986) *Sei autori in cerca di personaggio*, Turin: Centro scientifico torinese.
Martín Cabré, L. (1994) 'Il contributo di Ferenczi al concetto di controtransfert', paper presented to the Tenth National Congress of the SPI, Rimini, October.
Meltzer, D. (1967) *The Psycho-Analytic Process*, London: Heinemann.
—— (1973) *Sexual States of Mind*, Strath Tay, Perthshire: Clunie Press.
—— (1976) 'Temperature and distance as technical dimensions of interpretation', in *Sincerity and Other Works: Collected Papers of Donald Meltzer*, London: Karnac, 1994.
—— (1982a) 'Interventi in allucinazione e bugia', *Quaderni di psicoterapia infantile*, 13: 161–87.
—— (1982b) 'Una indagine sulle bugie: loro genesi e relazione con l'allucinazione', *Quaderni di psicoterapia infantile*, 13: 188–92.

—— (1982c) 'Verità della mente e bugia nella vita del sogno', *Quaderni di Psicoterapia Infantile*, 13.

—— (1984) *Dream-Life: A Re-Examination of the Psycho-Analytic Theory and Technique*, London: Karnac.

—— (1986) *Studies in Extended Metapsychology*, London: Karnac.

Meotti, A. and Meotti, F. (1996) 'Gruppo interno, identificazioni multiple e trasmissione transgenerazionale: problemi di tecnica dell'interpretazione', *Convegno a seminari multipli*, Bologna.

Merini, A. (1995) *Sogno e poesia*, Milan: La vita felice.

Miller, J. Hillis (1980) 'Theory and practice: response to Vincent Leitch', *Clinical Inquiry*, 6: 609–14.

Muñoz, M.L. (1998) 'Las mil caras del sufrimiento psíquico infantil y la respuesta del psicoanálisis', paper presented at the Cursos de Verano de la Fundación General, Universidad Complutense de Madrid, L'Escorial, August.

Musatti, C. (1949) *Trattato di psicoanalisi*, Turin: Bollati Boringhieri.

Neri, C. (1993) 'Campo e fantasie transgenerazionali', *Rivista di Psicoanalisi*, 39: 43–64.

—— (1995) *Gruppo*, Rome: Borla.

—— (1997) 'Commutare-commuovere'. Transiti dal gruppo all'individuo e viceversa', in E. Gaburri (ed.) *Emozione e interpretazione*, Turin: Bollati Boringhieri.

Nissim Momigliano, L. (1991) 'The psychoanalyst in the mirror: doubts galore, but few certainties', *International Journal of Psychoanalysis*, 72: 287–96.

—— (1992) *Continuity and Change in Psychoanalysis: Letters from Milan*, London: Karnac.

Norman, J. (1993) 'Frequency in child and adolescent analysis', *Psychoanalysis in Europe*, 41: 60–4.

—— (1995) 'Conflicts about interpretation: what, when and how to interpret?', *Psychoanalysis in Europe*, 45: 27–41.

Nosek, L. (1995) 'A aprensão teórica da realidade psíquica: a metapsicología freudiana', in *Fórum de Psicanálise*, São Paulo: Sociedade Brasileira de Psicanálise de São Paulo.

Olmos de Paz, T. (1990) 'De la confusión a la simbolización: adolescencia y proceso psicoanalítico', paper read at the Madrid Psychoanalytical Association.

—— (1996) 'Adolescencia: en los límites de lo analizable', *Revista de Psicoanálisis*, 24: 183.

—— (1998) 'Dolor mental en adolescencia y cura psicoanalítica', paper presented at the Cursos de Verano de la Fundación General, Universidad Complutense de Madrid, L'Escorial, August.

Propp, V. (1928) *Morphology of the Folktale*, trans. L. Scott, Bloomington, IN: Research Center, Indiana University.

Racker, H. (1969) *Estudios sobre técnica psicoanalítica*, Buenos Aires: Paidós.

Renik, O. (1993a) 'Countertransference enactment and the psychoanalytic process', in M.J. Horowitz, O.F. Kernberg and E.M. Weinshel (eds) *Psychic Structure and Psychic Change: Essays in Honor of Robert S. Wallerstein, M.D.*, Madison, CT: International Universities Press.

—— (1993b) 'Analytic interaction: conceptualizing technique in the light of the analyst's irreducible subjectivity', *Psychoanalytic Quarterly*, 62: 553–71.

Renik, O. (1998) 'The analyst's subjectivity and the analyst's objectivity', *International Journal of Psychoanalysis*, 79: 487–98.

Resnik, S. (1982) *The Theatre of the Dream*, trans. A. Sheridan, London: Tavistock.
—— (1986) *L'esperienza psicotica*, Turin: Bollati Boringhieri.
—— (1998) 'Narcisismo e depressione nell'analisi di pazienti psicotici', Seminario presso la Clinica Psichiatrica, University of Pavia, March.
Riolo, F. (1986) 'Dei soggetti del campo: un discorso sui limiti', *Gruppo e Funzione Analitica*, 7: 195–203.
—— (1989) 'Teoria delle trasformazioni', *Gruppo e Funzione Analitica*, 10: 7–41.
—— (1997) 'Il modello di campo in psicoanalisis', in E. Gaburri (ed.) *Emozione e interpretazione*, Turin: Bollati Boringhieri.
Robutti, A. (1992a) 'Introduction', in L. Nissim Momigliano and A. Robutti (eds) *Shared Experience: The Psychoanalytic Dialogue*, London: Karnac.
—— (1992b) 'Cassandra: a myth for hypochondria', in L. Nissim Momigliano and A. Robutti (eds) *Shared Experience: The Psychoanalytic Dialogue*, London: Karnac.
Rocha Barros, E.M. (1992) 'Escrita psicanalítica e prática clínica', *Revista Brasileira de Psicanálise*, 26: 205–11.
—— (1994) 'A interpretação: seus pressupostos teóricos', *Revista de Psicanálise*, SPPA, 1: 57–72.
—— (1996) 'Addressing the psychic reality of the borderline child', *International Journal of Psychoanalysis*, 77: 107–10.
—— (1997) 'O processo criativo e seus entraves à elaboração da situação edipiana', *Revista de Psicanálise da SPPA*, 4: 273–87.
Rorty, R. (1989) *Contingency, Irony, and Solidarity*, Cambridge: Cambridge University Press.
Rosenfeld, H. (1987) *Impasse and Interpretation*, London: Tavistock.
Rothstein, A. (ed.) (1985) *Models of the Mind: Their Relationships to Clinical Work*, New York: International Universities Press.
Sacco, F. (1995a) 'Bref parcours historique', in *Le Dessin dans la séance psychanalytique*, Ramonville-Saint-Agne: Erès.
—— (1995b) 'De l'agir à la mise en forme, ou le destin du figurable', in *Le Dessin dans la séance psychanalytique*, Ramonville-Saint-Agne: Erès.
Sandler, J. (1976) 'Countertransference and role responsiveness', *International Review of Psychoanalysis*, 3: 43–7.
Sapienza, A. (1995) 'Sexualidade e psicanálise: mapeando vínculos emocionais primitivos através de um sonho', in *Forum de Psicanálise*, Sociedade Brasileira de Psicanálise de São Paulo.
Schacht, L. (1995) 'Between child and adult analysis: creative moments of linking in the analyst's mind', *Psychoanalysis in Europe*, 45: 68–74.
Semi, A.A. (1998) 'Sogno e storie', Eleventh National Congress of the SPI, Rome, June.
Siniavsky, M. (1980) 'Acerca de la identidad del analista de niños y su ruptura y deserción', *Revista de la Asociación Psicoanalítica de Buenos Aires, Psicoanálisis, Técnica psicoanalítica*, 2: 1229–38.
Spence, D.P. (1982) *Narrative Truth and Historical Truth: Meaning and Interpretation in Psychoanalysis*, New York: Norton.
Speziale-Bagliacca, R. (1982) *On the Shoulders of Freud: Freud, Lacan, and the Psychoanalysis of Phallic Ideology*, New Brunswick, NJ: Transaction, 1991.
—— (1991) 'The capacity to contain: notes on its function in psychic change', *International Journal of Psychoanalysis*, 72: 27–33.

—— (1998) *Guilt: Revenge, Remorse and Responsibility after Freud*, trans. I. Harvey, New York: Brunner-Routledge, 2004.

Spillius, E. Bott (1983) 'Some developments from the work of Melanie Klein', *International Journal of Psychoanalysis*, 64: 321–32.

—— (1988) *Melanie Klein Today*, London: Routledge.

Stevenson, R.L. (1892) 'A chapter on dreams', in *Across the Plains*, Freeport, NY: Books for Libraries Press, 1972.

—— (1902a) 'The persons of the tale', in *Fables by Robert Louis Stevenson with Six Etchings by Ethel King Martyn*, London: Longmans Green.

—— (1902b) 'The reader', in *Fables by Robert Louis Stevenson with Six Etchings by Ethel King Martyn*, London: Longmans Green.

Tuckett, D. (1989) 'A brief view of Herbert Rosenfeld's contribution to the theory of psychoanalytical technique', *International Journal of Psychoanalysis*, 70: 619–25.

Uchoa Junqueira Filho, L.C. (1995) 'Realidade psíquica', in *Fórum de Psicanálise*, São Paulo: Sociedade Brasileira de Psicanálise de São Paulo.

Vallino Macciò, D. (1992) 'Surviving, existing, living: reflections on the analyst's anxiety', in L. Nissim Momigliano and A. Robutti (eds) *Shared Experience: The Psychoanalytic Dialogue*, London: Karnac.

—— (1997) 'Il campo psicoanalitico e il giardino segreto: una metafora per lo sviluppo del pensiero vivente', in E. Gaburri (ed.) *Emozione e interpretazione*, Turin: Bollati Boringhieri.

Waksman, J. (1985) 'La controtransferencia del analista de niños', *Revista de la Asociación Psicoanalítica de Buenos Aires, Psicoanálisis de niños y adolescentes*, 2: 551–72.

Winnicott, D.W. (1971) *Playing and Reality*, London: Tavistock.

Zac de Goldstein, R. (1984) 'The dark continent and its enigmas', *International Journal of Psychoanalysis*, 65: 179–89.

Index

For Product Safety Concerns and Information please contact our EU
representative GPSR@taylorandfrancis.com
Taylor & Francis Verlag GmbH, Kaufingerstraße 24, 80331 München, Germany

www.ingramcontent.com/pod-product-compliance
Ingram Content Group UK Ltd.
Pitfield, Milton Keynes, MK11 3LW, UK
UKHW020207200926
475702UK00004B/646

* 9 7 8 0 4 1 5 3 7 2 0 4 6 *